Speaking with
a Purpose

Fourth Edition

Speaking with a Purpose

Arthur Koch
Milwaukee Area Technical College

Allyn and Bacon
Boston • London • Toronto • Sydney • Tokyo • Singapore

Vice President, Humanities: Paul Smith
Developmental Editor: Carol Alper
Series Editorial Assistant: Kathy Rubino
Composition Buyer: Linda Cox
Manufacturing Buyer: Suzanne Lareau
Cover Administrator: Linda Knowles
Production Administrator: Rosalie Briand
Editorial-Production Service: Spectrum Publisher Services

Library of Congress Cataloging-in-Publication Data

Koch, Arthur.
    Speaking with a purpose / Arthur Koch.—4th ed.
      p. cm.
    Includes index.
    ISBN 0–205–27301–7 (pbk. : alk. paper)
    1. Public speaking. I. Title.
PN5121.K63   1997   97–11119
  808.5′1–dc21   CIP

Printed in the United States of America

10 9 8 7 6 5 4   01 00 99

For Jeremy, Carl, Debra, and all victims of mental illness

Contents

Preface

Speaking with a Purpose is a brief introduction to speechmaking, based primarily on a traditional public speaking approach. It is designed to aid beginning speakers in developing the skills they need to prepare and deliver effective speeches.

Numerous benefits await the person who can communicate successfully through speech. Improved self-concept, increased confidence, greater employability, and the ability to get along better with others are just a few of these benefits.

After thirty years of teaching speech to undergraduate students and business and professional people, I am convinced that the best way to learn the skill of speaking effectively is by preparing, practicing, and presenting speeches. For this reason I have intentionally written a text brief enough to allow the reader more time for involvement in the speechmaking process rather than in lengthy examination of theory.

Although *Speaking with a Purpose* presents up-to-date communication theory, it follows a step-by-step approach to preparing and delivering speeches. The text contains numerous examples excerpted from actual speeches chosen to represent a broad range of interests. As the title suggests, purpose and audience response are emphasized throughout the text.

The arrangement of the book is logical. Chapter 1 discusses the importance of speech, guidelines to successful speechmaking, nervousness, the speech communication process, and listening. Chapters 2 through 9 follow an eight-step approach on how to prepare and deliver a successful speech, highlighting the importance of combining personal knowledge and experience with modern technology. Chapter 10 covers speaking to inform and Chapter 11 involves an in-depth study of persuasion and persuasive speaking.

A feature of Chapter 12—the group communication chapter—is the inclusion of case problems as topics for discussion. These human relations problems, which involve situations that discussants are likely to encounter in everyday life, have proven effective in stimulating group participation.

Speech and discussion evaluation forms, audience analysis guides, and specific speaking assignments are included at the end of each chapter.

Whereas all chapters in the third edition appear in this fourth edition, some have been revised extensively. Chapter 2 has been updated and the section on the central idea has been greatly expanded. The segment on visual aids in Chapter 4 has been enlarged. Chapter 5 has been redesigned to stress the importance of electronic resources and the Internet when doing research for a speech. Chapter 7 has been modified to present five objectives to consider when planning a speech introduction, specific instructions on how to develop a comprehensive planning outline, and a sample outline for study. A sample full-sentence outline for a speech to instruct has been added to Chapter 10.

I wish to thank Charles E. Albrecht, Waukesha County Technical College; Sharon Askew, Virginia State University; Ginger DeBow-Makino, San Joaquin Delta College; James Highland, Daley College; Joel Patterson, DeVry Institute of Technology; and Deborah S. Workman, Myers College, for their valuable comments and suggestions in reviewing this book. I am indebted to Marian Tyndale Carter, Crafton Hills College, California, for her input and for her section on controlling nervousness and developing confidence in Chapter 1.

I am also indebted to the many people connected with Allyn and Bacon who have made this new edition possible. I especially thank Carol Alper, Project Manager, and Rosalie Briand, Senior Production Assistant, both of Allyn and Bacon, and Kelly Ricci, Production Manager of Spectrum Publisher Services.

Arthur Koch

1

Getting Started

In today's society, the person who can't communicate operates under a severe handicap. One of the main reasons employees lose their jobs is not that they lack the skill to do them but that they are unable to communicate effectively with their fellow workers. We constantly hear of the communication gap between government and citizens, between children and parents, between teachers and students, and between husbands and wives.

According to Dr. J. Ross Eshelman, chairman of the department of social psychology at Wayne State University, "Although there are a multitude of reasons given for divorce, such as adultery, drunkenness, sexual problems, and the like, in most cases these are problems caused by an inability of the marriage partners to communicate with each other."

What this all adds up to is obvious. If you want to get along better with others and if you want to be more successful in life, you will improve your chances considerably by learning to communicate more effectively.

You will undoubtedly be called upon to make speech presentations at various times in your life: as a student participating in a classroom symposium; as an employee presenting a description of the company you work for to a community group; as a concerned citizen addressing a legislative committee on some social issue. In each of these situations, your ability to say something worthwhile effectively will enhance your presentation considerably. People tend to equate ability to speak well with ability to think well. Every time you speak you are communicating something about who you are to others. If you want others to see you as an effective speaker, two broad guidelines can help ensure success: (1) say something worthwhile, and (2) say it in an easy, natural way.

Say Something Worthwhile

When you prepare a speech, you are concerned with two things: what you want to say, and how you want to say it. What you say is called the content of your speech, which includes your subject, main idea and supporting material, organization, and the way you word your speech. Whenever you can, you should choose a worthwhile subject from your own area of interest so that you are familiar with what you are talking about and have some concern for your subject. Next, you must develop the subject with your audience in mind. An audience will pay attention to something that is either useful or interesting to them. If you can show your audience that your subject is useful to them, this will give them a reason to pay attention. Point out how your speech will be useful to your listeners in the introduction. If your subject is interesting to them, you can get their attention in the introduction and hold it throughout the speech.

If, however, your subject does not seem useful to your audience, is not interesting of itself, yet you still want to choose it because you feel it is worthwhile, in order to hold their attention you must make it interesting to them. Suggestions for getting and holding the attention of your audience are found in Chapter 7. Keep in mind that the less interesting or useful a subject is, the more difficult it will be to hold the audience's attention. For example, unless you were in a class of art students an informative speech on Salvador Dali's contribution to modern art would take a lot more imagination and effort to make interesting to a typical audience than a speech on the Beatle's influence on rock and roll.

Similarly, your listeners would be more likely to see the usefulness of a speech on the effects of alcohol on the mind and body than on one demonstrating how to make an arrow. Almost everyone takes a drink now and then or knows someone who does, perhaps taking more than he or she should. Knowing what the positives and negatives of drinking alcohol are would most likely seem useful to many. On the other hand, knowing how to make an arrow would probably only seem useful to a bow hunter or avid archer.

This does not mean, however, that a speech demonstrating how to make an arrow could not be made interesting to a general audience. A number of years ago, one of my students, a Native American from a Wisconsin Chippewa tribe, delivered a speech on how to make an arrow. He brought in a modern apparatus for aligning the feathers and the arrowhead on the arrow shaft, so that the arrow would be in perfect balance. He showed us a variety of modern arrows and bows. Then he showed us a number of bows and arrows that had been made by the members of his or other Ojibwa tribes over one hundred fifty years earlier. The arrowheads were flint and the feathers had come from eagles or hawks. When he put the primitive arrows on the apparatus they were way out of balance. The bows were obviously nowhere near as powerful as the ones made today. He explained that Indians wore moccasins and learned to walk without making a sound so that they could get close enough to hit whatever they were stalking with their primitive weapons. The speech was interesting and informative. It cleared up some misconceptions the class had from watching cowboy and Indian movies and gave the class a greater appreciation of the contributions and resourcefulness of Native Americans.

Say It in an Easy Way

The way you say something is called delivery. Delivery includes such things as eye contact, facial expression, body movement, personal appearance, and voice. Effective delivery should seem confident and natural. Besides an increase in volume for a larger audience, there are a number of differences between platform speaking and ordinary conversation. First, platform speaking is intentional. As the title of this text emphasizes, a speech is delivered with a clear purpose in mind. Second, a speech is more carefully prepared than everyday conversation. A subject is chosen and developed with a specific audience in mind and words are chosen more carefully. If you want to deliver an effective speech, you must be clear about what you want to say and whom you are trying to reach. Remember, in most cases, the only interaction with your audience that you have in a speech situation is their nonverbal response.

Your delivery will seem more confident and natural if you use a conversational style. A conversational style makes frequent use of the personal pronoun, which gives it an air of familiarity, as if the speaker were talking to close friends. Use your own vocabulary but eliminate words that might be considered overly casual or inappropriate. If you try to use words with which you are unfamiliar, your style will seem stilted and unnatural. You should, however, choose your words carefully. Keep in mind: Speech is more formal than ordinary conversation, and your language should be a bit more formal too.

The advantage of using your own vocabulary when delivering a speech is that you will feel more natural and comfortable. Talking about something you feel is important and about which you are sincere will help you exude confidence.

At this point, you might be asking yourself, "How can I exude confidence, when the thought of giving a speech gives my stomach butterflies?"

The Truth about Nervousness*

Nervousness is learned behavior. Several years ago in a psychology class called "Self-Confidence," a young mother brought her four-year-old son to

*Material on pages 3–9 is taken with permission from Marian Tyndale Carter, *Content and Delivery* 2nd ed (Beaumont, CA: Maple Leaf Publishing Co., 1995).

the final exam class because of a mix-up with a sitter. The final exam was a short talk about some of the ideas learned in the class and how they had made life better. There were eighteen students in the class and as we listened to the talks we heard people sharing many wonderful changes that they had created in their own feelings, in their relationships, and in their school and career successes. The group was very supportive and warmly applauded each speaker. When the last student finished, the little boy slipped off his chair and went to the front of the group. He said, "I want to talk." He then talked for one to two minutes about his dog, how they played and how happy his dog made him feel. The applause was loud and there were quite a few of us with suspiciously bright eyes. When he went back to his mother, we all heard him say, "That was fun. I liked it." I have never forgotten this precious child who had never learned to be afraid of standing in front of an audience. I was so impressed that, first of all, he perceived the caring and connection that was experienced as these students shared of themselves and were acknowledged lovingly by their classmates. He knew this was a good thing and he wanted to experience it. Second, even this young child perceived accurately that the speakers were telling about things in their own lives and sharing their emotional feelings, so he just unself-consciously shared something important from his life and the emotions he felt of happiness. Right on target! I have often pondered the possible results if we could but teach public speaking to young children before they learn to be so afraid.

Public speaking is probably the course feared by more students than any other. The reasons for this fear are numerous and not all negative. However, in my experience, many students have horror stories to tell about being laughed at or humiliated in elementary school. This particular fear usually yields quite easily to the confidence-building sequence of easy speaking activities in the early part of the semester. The positive feedback from classmates and from your own videotaped performances is very powerful and when supplemented with positive self-talk is very effective in replacing those fears from childhood. A more appropriate or rational nervousness is created because you care about what the audience thinks about you. This is especially true when you stand before a group of your peers. This concern for the opinion of your fellow human beings is appropriate if not carried too far. Appropriate caring causes you to do all you can to do your best. It gives you the extra rush of energy that you need to be really alive in front of an audience. Albert Ellis said in his book *A New Guide to Rational Living* that 98% of our anxiety is *overconcern* about what others will think of us. Overconcern is then the problem. Overconcern is usually stimulated and reinforced by negative self-talk such as, "I'm so nervous!," "I can't do this!," "I know I'll forget everything!," or that old classic self-fulfilling prophecy, "When I get in front of an audience my mind goes blank!" Say any of these affirmations enough and they tend to become the truth. Your strongest "word of honor" seems to be that spoken of yourself to yourself!

One really fascinating view of nervousness is that on a physiological level the physical signs of nervousness parallel the physical signs of excitement. That is to say that two people may experience the same symptoms and one may name it nervousness and the other may name it excitement. I urge every student to rename their nervous feelings sincerely as *excitement* and see how that changes their perception of their feelings.

For several semesters I had students rank themselves as speakers and the audience rank the speaker in terms of how nervous they were. We used a scale of zero to twenty. It was quite consistent that the speaker perceived himself to be twice as nervous as the audience would perceive him to be. That is, if a speaker said he was an eighteen on the nervousness scale, the audience on the average would perceive him to be right close to nine on that same scale. It is reassuring to realize that as a speaker a person only appears half as nervous to the audience as he thinks he appears.

Developing Self-Confidence

As the oft-quoted saying, "Nothing succeeds like success," implies, the experience of doing well in the speech activities in class will go a long way toward helping you develop greater self-confidence. To this end always talk about something you really know, prepare, and practice very well. Be sincere and talk about things that really matter to you. Never, never try to "con" an audience into believing that you know something you do not. You cannot fool an audience. They can almost always tell exactly how much you do or do not know, how much time you have spent preparing, and above all how much time you spent rehearsing. Being well prepared and well rehearsed create almost certain success. This is what builds confidence.

Physically there are several very important things you can do to build self-confidence. First, be sure that you do not form the habit of holding your breath or breathing very shallowly. Many people, without even realizing it, breathe less deeply or even hold their breath when they experience stress. This can really backfire, as it can diminish the flow of oxygen to the brain which may trigger a fear response which is mistaken for nervousness, not a physical reaction to lack of oxygen. Posture is also very important in developing self-confidence. If you stand with your weight evenly balanced on both feet, spine erect, head up, and arms loose at your side, your body will experience balance and comfort. If you stand with weight all on one foot with the opposite hip stuck outward (often called "hip-shot") with spine curved, shoulders humped, head forward, eyes down, your body will experience feelings of vulnerability and lack of safety because the body is off balance and it is easy to push you over in this posture. So the posture signals you send to your own body and mind are very important. Another important physiological warning for speakers is never lock your knees while you are giving a speech. Locking your knees results in blocking major circulation pathways. In certain situations, such as under the hot sun while standing at attention, locking your knees could cause you to pass out. While speaking, it would probably cause your legs to tremble, thus creating the appearance and feeling of nervousness.

Psychologically there are several very important steps you can take to develop greater self-confidence. You can practice positive self-talk, repeatedly saying to yourself with as much conviction as you can create, "I can do this," "I can take it one step at a time," "I can become an excellent speaker," "This class is getting easier every week," and "I really want to learn to be a powerful speaker!" A second physiological exercise is to banish all talk of fear and nervousness. Substitute other less loaded words when you talk of your concerns. From now on instead of "I'm really nervous," say "I'm really excited." If you are compelled to acknowledge your previous levels of nervousness, always say "In the past I have had some problems with nervousness, but it is getting better all of the time." Such relanguaging or renaming something is a powerful way to gain control over your psychological reactions. Constantly using "I am very excited," and eliminating the fear and nervousness talk is a powerful technique for changing your whole response pattern to the public speaking situation. In order for this to be effective in lessening nervousness, you do not have to believe strongly in your positive self-talk, but you *do* have to eliminate negative self-talk, or the positive and negative statements will cancel each other, leaving you to experience little growth in this area.

Another very powerful psychological idea is to change your focus from concern for yourself to concern for the audience. All too often a speaker is so focused on the impression he is making that he forgets to be really focused on how well the audience is hearing, seeing, understanding, and so forth. When your attention is turned back upon yourself, your mind will be filled with questions like, " Do I look scared?," "Do I sound stupid?," "What if I forget?," "Can they see my knees shaking?," and on and on. The speaker who can forget himself and really be concerned if the audience is understanding the very important ideas he is sharing will experience a genuine shift to a nurturing connection with the audience. This is the feeling that causes many a speaker to get "hooked" on public speaking. It is a very powerful feeling when you realize that you can share an idea that could change someone's life. This can only happen if you talk about things that are so very interesting and important to you that you truly want every person in the audience to understand. This means preparing well and working on that shift of focus. I have seen speakers experience this shift of focus and when they had that experience, it eliminated most of their excessive nervousness.

Stretch Your Comfort Zone

Your comfort zone is defined by your self-concept, your family culture, your community and national culture, and so on. As long as you are not violating any of the "rules" of any of these belief systems you are in your comfort zone. Some of these "rules" are appropriate but many are just habits handed down which end up creating a big rut which controls the direction of our life more than most of us realize. A more general approach to building confidence is to look constantly for opportunities to stretch your comfort zone in every area of life. If you are more comfortable waiting for someone else to speak first, push yourself to speak first as often as possible. Be on the lookout for little ways you can stretch that comfort zone. Push yourself in class. Ask more questions in stores. Ask for information. Try dressing differently. Seek leadership roles. Volunteer some time at the library literacy program. Go to a town council meeting and ask a question. Take voice lessons. Take flying lessons. Go horseback riding. Drive somewhere you have never been. Challenge yourself to be aware and to act by choice, not by habit. Try out for a role in a community theater play.

Visual Imagery Is a Powerful Tool

The next delivery topic is a visual imagery technique specifically for developing confidence in public speaking. Mental rehearsal is another name for visual imagery. This technique is a fascinating tool for changing behavior and the same procedure presented on the next few pages can be adapted to create behavior change in any area of life. You could even use it to practice remembering more and scoring better on the quizzes and to stop procrastinating and do that paperwork and other preparation early. Be creative and see how many areas you can find to try the three-step method of visual imagery you are now going to learn.

Visual Imagery for Confidence in Public Speaking

Visual imagery for behavior change is a powerful technique which gained broad exposure during the Olympic Games in Los Angeles. In TV interviews, sports coaches of a wide variety of different events explained how this technique, used as a *regular* part of daily practice, had helped athletes to improve their performances. From divers to gymnasts, visual imagery was found to be a valuable tool.

The subconscious mind does not seem to differentiate between actual physical rehearsal and mental rehearsal (visual imagery) when the mental rehearsal is done with the same concentration and vivid feelings associated with the actual physical rehearsal. The benefits from mental rehearsal done well are many. The rehearsal is completely under the control of the person doing the imagery, therefore each rehearsal can be a positive, strengthening experience. The time involved is much less than actual practice requires, therefore more practice can be done. The troublesome spots in an activity can be practiced over and over easily. The subconscious mind can build a store-house of "success" feelings about an activity. These feelings then encourage continued successful performance just as actual successful rehearsal would.

The visual imagery pattern I recommend for speech students desiring to experience more confidence and greater speaking skill in front of an audience is a simple three-step pattern. It is suggested that you practice using this pattern (or your own personal version of it) at least three times a day. Each session should be brief (two to five minutes) but as intensely vivid and "real" as you can create it. Do this brief visual imagery three or more times a day for two to three weeks or longer and you will find a tremendous development of skill and confidence is the result. Each session should take only two to three minutes. Visual imagery can be done any place where you can be uninterrupted for a few minutes. The very best schedule is morning, midday, and evening. Detailed instructions for using the visual imagery pattern described above follow.

For a more in-depth discussion of visual imagery you will enjoy reading the books *Psycho-Cybernetics* by Maxwell Maltz, *Visualization* by Adelaide Bry, *The Mind's Eye* by Arnold Lazarus, *Creative Visualization* by Shakti Gawain, and *Visualization for Change* by Patrick Fanning. There are also some subliminal tapes available which seem to help some people develop greater confidence in public speaking.

A Script for Using Visual Imagery to Develop Confidence in Speaking

Step One: Systematic Relaxation

Pay particular attention to shoulders, face, and stomach muscles. The purpose of step one is to focus attention away from your outer environment onto your physical body, then relax your body sufficiently to avoid its becoming a distraction later in the process when you focus your attention within yourself. Sit in a centered posture—do not recline. Start with your toes and systematically relax every part of your body up to the very top of your head. Tensing and relaxing is good if at first your shoulders or other large muscle groups are very tense.

Step Two: Favorite Peaceful Place

Picture a vivid sensory-rich scene in nature. You should use this same scene over and over or at least until you change projects. I usually use the beach.

Focus on all the sensory details possible—sky, water, waves, sunlight, sun's warmth, sounds of birds and water, feel of sand underfoot, and so on. See yourself walking along the beach experiencing the colors, sights, sounds, touches, and freedom of the beach as vividly as you can.

Step Three: Rehearsing Your Desired Behavior

Picture yourself doing the behavior you desire to do just as perfectly as you hope to learn to do it—speaking with confidence and skill. The sequence I recommend is to see yourself sitting at your desk, aware that you are the next speaker. When it is your turn you rise confidently and walk to the podium. You look confidently at individuals in the audience, then begin with a ringing powerful opening statement. See yourself standing and speaking with real authority and clarity. You do not have to "hear" any actual words. Feel the energy and enthusiasm in your delivery. See people in the audience nodding their heads in agreement with your ideas. Feel your strong desire to communicate the interest and the importance of the information you are sharing. See yourself finishing with a strong dynamic ending statement. Hear the loud spontaneous applause as your audience acknowledges your excellent speech. Notice how you really enjoy the feeling of having done a good job. Feel this enjoyment. This is a very important ingredient in the visualization—your enjoyment of your success. See yourself now returning to your seat with the same sincere and confident attitude. See yourself sitting with a big smile on your face—very pleased with yourself. Enjoy and strengthen this feeling for a few moments before you open your eyes and are finished with the session.

The Communicative Act

Five elements are involved in the speech communication process: a speaker, a message, a channel (through which the message is sent), an audience, and a response. Each time a speaker communicates a message to others, these elements are present. In speaking situations these elements interact with each other. A simple speech situation can be summarized as follows:

1. A speaker wishes to communicate an idea.
2. The speaker encodes the idea in a message.
3. The message is sent through a channel to an audience.
4. The audience receives and decodes the message.
5. The audience responds to the message.

As you can see, the communication process is complex. In order to understand it better, it might be helpful to consider each of the five elements in the process separately.

Speaker

In the previous model, the process of communication begins with a speaker who wishes to communicate an idea or some ideas. The image that the audience has of the speaker affects the message. Those in the audience who perceive a speaker as being a person of competence, integrity, and goodwill are most likely to believe what the speaker says.

Message

The second element in the communication process is the message. In order to ensure that the listener attends to the message and understands it, the speaker must encode it in language that is both interesting and clear. Emphasis, variety, and descriptive language help make material interesting. Words that are specific and familiar help to make a message clear.

Channel

The channel is the means through which a message is transmitted. In the speaking situation the channel can involve all the senses through which each member of the audience receives the information. Messages can be transmitted through hearing, seeing, smelling, tasting, and touching channels. A speaker can choose words that appeal to the audience's five senses, can include sensory aids in the message, or can add nonverbals to the message to make it more meaningful.

Audience

Without an audience, communication does not take place. A person stranded on an island can put a note in a bottle or stand on the shore screaming for help. However, unless someone reads the note or hears the screams, nothing will have been accomplished. This emphasizes the fact that all communication by a speaker must be audience centered. Unless a message is encoded with a specific audience in mind, it is liable to fail.

Response

In the final analysis, the success or failure of a communication is determined by audience response. The title of this book, *Speaking with a Purpose*, underlines the fact that in order to be successful when communicating, the speaker's purpose—to inform, to entertain, or to persuade—must be achieved. Therefore, the success or failure of a communication is measured by whether or not those in the audience are informed, entertained, or persuaded.

Communication Breakdowns

Communication breakdowns occur because of some failure in the communication process. If you invite a friend to your house for a Friday night fish fry and she comes Thursday night, the message you gave her was either inaccurate or misunderstood. If because you were daydreaming you fail to hear your instructor announce that the next class meeting has been called off, you might be the only class member present on that day. Communication breakdowns occur at some point during the speech situation. Perhaps the speaker has failed to analyze the audience correctly. Maybe the message has been encoded in technical terms that the audience cannot understand. Or it might be that the microphone the speaker is using significantly distorts the message. Any of these factors could result in a breakdown of communication.

Usually communication breakdowns can be traced to one of the five elements in the communication process: the speaker, message, channel, audience, or response. Consider the following situations and determine where the breakdowns in communication occurred.

1. Some of the members of your audience fail to understand parts of your speech on computer database technology because of the terminology you use. (Remember, you are most likely talking to a general audience. What is clear to those who are computer literate might seem like gibberish to those who are not.)
2. What you are wearing draws attention to itself, interfering with your message. (The clothes you wear should not distract or detract from what you are saying. Dressing too flamboyantly or too casually can conflict with what you are saying.)
3. The overhead projector you brought to show your charts malfunctions. (A good rule of thumb when planning to use visual aids in a speech is be prepared to do without them if need be. An audience will admire the speaker who is able to do this.)
4. The room you are speaking in is large and it is difficult for those in the back to hear you. (If you haven't checked this out beforehand, you can only ask those in the back to move forward or increase your volume.)
5. Some type of external noise interferes with your audience's ability to hear you. (Remain silent until the noise stops. Unless your audience can hear you, communication is not taking place.)

Listening

It is a frustrating thought that while you are delivering your speech, chances are that less than 15 percent of your audience will be actively listening to you.

Most of them will be hearing you but not really listening. There is a considerable difference between hearing and listening. Hearing is the act of perceiving sounds, while listening involves making sense out of what you have heard.

Listening is an active process involving both concentration and thinking. Ineffective listening usually occurs because of a breakdown in one of these two areas. Often there is a barrier that interferes with the listener's concentration or the person has never learned to listen properly. Following are eight barriers to concentration in listening:

Barriers to Listening

External Noise

External noise includes noises both inside and outside the listening area. Talking, footsteps, whispering, coughing, and street noise are some of the things that make it difficult to pay attention to a speaker. As a listener, you can avoid such distractions by arriving early enough at a speech or lecture to get a seat where you can see and hear easily. As a speaker, you can aid your audience by remaining silent until an emergency vehicle passes by or a bell stops ringing.

Internal Noise

Sometimes inner distractions caused by personal problems or concern about others can be so intense that it is extremely difficult to listen carefully. This internal "noise" can often be more distracting than a baby crying. When you are concerned about an upcoming test, a broken relationship, or a similar concern, you must redouble your efforts to concentrate.

Bias toward Speaker

If a speaker's voice or appearance or mannerisms annoy you, listening carefully will become difficult. An instructor whose voice is raspy, who paces the floor, or who prefaces everything with "you know" can make a semester seem like an eternity. Work to overcome this listening barrier by concentrating on the content of the speech rather than the delivery.

Emotional Reaction

Sometimes a word or phrase can cause a negative response that can interfere with a listener's ability to concentrate. Loaded words like *honky* or *greaser* or the use of profanity can trigger emotional responses that interfere with a person's ability to listen effectively. Try to screen out emotional reactions by resolving to hear everything a speaker has to say before making a judgment.

Daydreaming

Who hasn't at one time or another drifted off into a pleasant daydream rather than pay attention? The tendency to daydream is influenced by two factors. First, a listener is able to think at a much faster rate than a speaker can speak. Consequently, while the speaker is talking at about 130 words per minute, the listener has plenty of thinking time left over. Second, attention is intermittent. That is, it stops and starts again at intervals. Daydreaming can be a serious barrier to listening. Learning to listen actively can help you avoid the tendency to daydream.

Faking Attention

Faking attention is a technique that is usually learned in the first or second grade. There students learn to sit at their desks while leaning forward with hands propped under their chins and an interested expression on their faces. Whether we learned it in school or not, we have all at one time or another been guilty of faking attention. The problem with faking attention is that it can be a difficult habit to break.

Fatigue

Listening is an active process that requires the energy of the listener. If you are tired from too much studying or partying the night before, you will find it difficult to concentrate on what the speaker is saying. If you know that you will be attending an important speech or lecture, make sure that you are well rested.

Improper Note Taking

Taking notes ineffectively is worse than not taking notes at all. Students who attempt to write down too much of what a speaker is saying often wind up missing the point the speaker is trying to make. The way to avoid this problem is to develop note-taking skills.

Ways to Improve Listening

Prepare to Listen

The first thing to do before attending a speech or lecture is to prepare yourself to listen. This means knowing something about the subject beforehand so that you can listen actively rather than passively. The first step in preparing to listen is to determine the subject from the title of the speech or lecture. Next you must think about what you already know about the subject. Chances are that you know something. If your knowledge is limited, you can go to the library or read your textbook to obtain information that will help you better understand what the speaker has to say. Preparing to listen is the first step to improving your listening skills. It is unlikely that you could listen with any degree of understanding to a subject you know "nothing" about.

Avoid Distractions

As indicated previously, distractions can interfere with concentration and make it difficult to listen. To limit external distractions, arrive early enough to get a centrally located seat close to the speaker. If that is impossible, avoid sitting near windows or an entrance or exit.

Internal distractions are harder to screen out. The fact that you are aware that you are being bothered by them should alert you to redouble your efforts to concentrate.

Identify the Central Idea

If the speech you are listening to has been well prepared, the central idea should be stated in the introduction. You might have already gotten a clue as to the central idea from the title. However, whether the speaker states the idea as a complete sentence or it is implicit in the message, as the listener you must be aware of what it is since the central idea is the main point of the speech.

Identify the Main Points

Most effective speeches involve a central idea supported by a number of main points. The listener's job is to sort out these main points from the supporting materials. This takes thinking and concentration. When identifying main points, listen for signals: "Some of the reasons that . . ." or "In addition . . ." Phrases like these tip you off to the fact that important ideas are forthcoming.

Think along with the Speaker

In order to listen actively you must think along with the speaker. As you are listening, try to reconstruct the organizational pattern of the speech. Determine if the speaker is supporting each new idea with a variety of supporting materials. Relate what the speaker is saying to your own knowledge and interests. Responding to the speech in this way will not only improve your active listening but will provide insights that will aid you in developing your own speeches.

Take Effective Notes

Learning to take effective notes is an excellent way to improve your listening skills. Note taking promotes active listening and concentration. Rather than just listening passively to a speaker, the note taker must listen with the mind in order to identify the speaker's important ideas. It takes clear thinking and concentration to sort out main ideas from supporting details.

Note-Taking Tips

Write down Only Important Ideas

A good speech is planned around a central idea and several main points. The central idea is usually stated in the introduction of the speech. Sometimes a speaker will also list in the introduction the main points to be covered. Listen for signals that indicate that main ideas are forthcoming. Words like *specifically, further,* and *first* indicate that a speaker is moving from one point to another.

Write Legibly

Sometimes note takers write so hurriedly that when they finish, they can't read their own notes. If your notes are illegible, you are probably writing down too much.

Keep up

If you find that you are falling behind in your note taking, skip a few lines and begin again. Later, when you expand your notes, you can fill in the missing information.

Use Your Own Words

One of the best ways to show that you understand something is to be able to explain it in your own words. When you translate the ideas of another into your own vocabulary, they will be easier to understand and remember.

Be Brief

A common mistake among inexperienced note takers is the tendency to write down too much. Don't try to write down everything the speaker says. A set of notes should be a summary of a speaker's main ideas.

Don't Erase

Rather than wasting time erasing, draw a line through the mistake and continue. Remember, the notes you are taking are for your own use. If you want your notes to be neat, you can rewrite or type them later.

Don't Worry about Spelling

If you're not sure about how a word is spelled, write it phonetically. You can check the spelling later when you expand your notes.

Date Your Notes

Whether you are taking notes on a lecture or a public speech, you should get into the habit of dating them. This will enable you to pinpoint a missed lecture or the specific date of a speech.

Expand Your Notes

If the notes you are taking are for the purpose of helping you remember information or to aid you in studying for an exam, it is wise to expand them as soon after a lecture as possible.

Exercises

1. Cite two examples of communication breakdowns. Indicate the causes of the breakdowns. Explain what could have been done to improve the communication in each case.
2. Tell of an instance when a barrier to listening kept you from concentrating at a speech or lecture. Did you try to overcome the barrier? What did you do?
3. List five areas where you could try the five-step method of visual imagery.
4. Do you have a favorite "peaceful place"? Describe it.
5. List an experience or experiences when you weren't nervous sharing something personal. List experiences when you were.

2

Determine Your Purpose and Subject

In order to develop an effective speech you must have a clear purpose in mind. The title of this book, *Speaking with a Purpose,* emphasizes the importance of purpose in oral communication. Your aim as a speaker should be to fulfill a purpose by achieving a desired response. Your success in informing, entertaining, or persuading must always be measured in terms of the response your receiver gives to your message. Beginning speakers often fail because they pay too little attention to purpose and audience response when planning their speeches. Following are the major purposes in speaking:

1. To entertain—to elicit a pleasurable response, to provoke curiosity, to provide suspense, or to amuse. Treating a serious subject lightly or a light subject seriously and describing an unusual or exciting experience are examples of communication to entertain.

2. To inform—to add to the knowledge or understanding of the listener. Demonstrating how to do something, explaining a process, reporting on a meeting, and describing an event are examples of communication to inform.

3. To persuade—to convince, to reinforce, or to actuate. Since persuasion is more complex than entertainment or information, the three types of persuasion will be treated separately.

   a. To convince—to change your listener's opinions or to commit them to a point of view about which they are undecided. Persuasion to convince occurs frequently in debate and in problem-solving discussion. In both, information is given to listeners in an attempt to get them to change their minds or to form an opinion on something about which they are undecided. Persuasion to convince relies heavily on a logical approach using reasoning, statistics, testimony, comparison, and factual examples.

b. To reinforce—to arouse and invigorate an audience already in agreement with the speaker's point of view. A speech at a pep rally in the school auditorium before a football or basketball game is a good example of persuasion to reinforce. The students do not have to be convinced about the importance of their team's winning. The idea is to strengthen their attitude about winning, to build a fire under them so that they are prepared emotionally and enthusiastically for the game. Persuasion to reinforce largely employs a psychological approach—appealing to the attitudes, beliefs, sentiments, and motives of the audience.

c. To actuate—to put into action. In the previous example the speaker's job is to stimulate the members of the student audience to become even more excited than they already are about the upcoming game. However, they are not given specific instructions as to what to do in terms of that excitement. In persuasion to actuate the audience should be told exactly what action you want accomplished. A speech by the coach to the team in the locker room before the game is a good example of persuasion to actuate. The team is told specifically to go out and "win one for the alma mater." The speech to actuate asks the audience to buy, to sell, to join, to march, or the like. While it can employ persuasion to convince or to reinforce or both, it is by far more successful when directed to an audience who already agrees. Obviously, if you want to get your audience to do something, you are bound to be more successful if it is already predisposed to act that way.

Selecting a Subject

Once you clearly understand the general purpose of your speech, you are ready to choose a subject. There will undoubtedly be times when you will be asked to deliver a speech on a topic that has already been determined. For example, you are asked to give a report on a convention you attended as a delegate. Or as a member of a symposium you are assigned to speak on one aspect of a subject. In a different situation the occasion might determine what your subject will be. However, more often than not, you will need to select your own subject. It may be that when you find you must deliver a speech, you immediately think of a subject you have interest in and which you feel will be interesting to your audience. If this happens, you can immediately begin developing your speech. However, if you can't think of an appropriate subject, take out a sheet of paper and write down as many things as you can that you are interested in or have experience with. There is no better place to look for a subject than in your own background. Did you grow up on a farm?

Did you come from a different part of the country? Where have you traveled? Do you have special skills in athletics, music, graphic arts, theater, or fashion design? What hobbies do you have? What are your political views? What issues turn you on? What do you talk about with close friends? With some imagination and hard work you can make these subjects interesting to your audience. When determining which subject to choose, ask yourself the following questions:

1. Is the subject suited to my purpose?
2. Is the subject interesting to me?
3. Am I qualified to speak on this subject?
4. Will my audience find this subject interesting?
5. Will my audience find this subject useful?
6. Is my subject sufficiently narrowed?

Is the Subject Suited to My Purpose?

Suppose you are asked to deliver a speech whose general purpose is to inform. Because you have recently began studying the U.S. Army School of the Americas in your Latin America history class, you decide to deliver an informative speech about this school, which was established in 1946 at Fort Benning, Georgia. As you begin developing the speech and find out more about the school, however, you learn that during the last fifty years, the School of the Americas has trained more than 87,000 Latin American and Caribbean soldiers, many of whom have committed some of the worst human rights violations in our hemisphere, and that officers who studied at the school are responsible for the torture, killing, and maiming of hundreds of thousands of innocent people in Latin America and that many graduates have destabilized democratic institutions or overthrown their governments. This would most likely give your listeners a highly negative view of this school which one Central American newspaper dubbed "School of the Assassins." This subject would be better suited as a speech with the general purpose to persuade and the specific purpose to actuate your audience to write their representative in Congress to support the Kennedy Bill, HR 2652 which will cut off funding for the School for the Americas, effectively closing it down.

Is the Subject Interesting to Me?

Whenever possible, choose a subject you find interesting. Enthusiasm is a key factor to successful speaking. If you talk enthusiastically about something, this enthusiasm is bound to rub off on your audience. Are you excited about a particular kind of music or art form? Are you into alternative rock or zydeco? Do you jog or lift weights? Collect coins? With a little imagination and some effort you can make what interests you interesting for your audience.

When you have difficulty finding a subject that interests you, try a technique called brainstorming. Take out a blank sheet of paper and jot down as many potential speech topics as you can. Don't worry about the quality of these topics; aim for quantity. After you have listed as many as you can, put the sheet away for at least eight hours. When you return to it, you may very well find that you have listed a number of topics of interest to you that you hadn't thought about.

Am I Qualified to Speak on This Subject?

What are your qualifications for dealing with a particular subject? The fact that you are interested in a subject does not necessarily mean that you are qualified to speak on it. If your interest is recent, you might lack sufficient knowledge or experience to prepare the subject effectively. In some cases it might be better to select a subject with which you are more familiar. Are you qualified because of background or skill? Do you speak from personal experience? What are your credentials? Do you have special skills in real estate, music, computers, or sewing? Sometimes the perfect speech topic is so close that the speaker doesn't see it. A speech by a student in the dental technology program on caring for your teeth will undoubtedly be well received by her classmates. If you have expertise or special knowledge or experience about your speech topic, indicate this to your audience in your introduction. If you have access to special information through a friend or relative who is an expert, indicate this as well. Even if your knowledge about the topic comes only through research, you want to let your audience know that what you are telling them is accurate and carefully prepared.

Will My Audience Find This Subject Interesting?

It takes little effort to pay attention to a subject that is interesting. Therefore you will hold the attention of your audience if your subject is interesting to them. If you are not sure it will be, you must work to make it so. An effective way to do this is to use attention factors—humor, novelty, suspense, and the like. You will find a discussion of attention factors on pages 69–73.

Will My Audience Find This Subject Useful?

People will willingly pay attention to a communication if they expect to gain something useful from doing so. Consider your own experience. Have you ever followed a set of instructions on how to operate a computer, bake a cake, or ferment your own wine? Have you ever attended a lecture on what to expect on the final exam? Have you ever bought a do-it-yourself book and tried to follow the "simplified instructions"? Did you pay attention? Of course you did. If the subject you choose will benefit your audience in some way, it will quite likely hold their attention. If you feel that the usefulness of your subject will not be readily apparent to your audience, tell them in your introduction how they will benefit from listening to your speech.

Is My Subject Sufficiently Narrowed?

In most cases you will be given a definite time limit when you are asked to give a speech. If you exceed this time limit appreciably you are bound to annoy your audience. Many beginning speakers try to cover too much in the time available to them. It is far better to deal with a restricted subject in detail than to cover too many points. Remember, if you cover too much material without supporting it adequately, your audience is unlikely to remember it no matter how long your speech is.

Specific Purpose

After you have chosen your subject in accordance with the considerations above, you are ready to formulate a specific purpose. Earlier I classified the general purposes for speaking: to entertain, to inform, and to persuade. Specific purposes tell more precisely what your intent is. They indicate in more detail exactly what you hope to accomplish. Note the following examples:

1. General purpose: to entertain
   Specific purposes:

   a. to amuse my audience by explaining how to wash a bull elephant
   b. to hold my audience in suspense while telling of the time I was robbed
   c. to amaze my audience with a demonstration of magic
   d. to fascinate my audience with a story about my first parachute jump

2. General purpose: to inform
   Specific purposes:

   a. to explain the art of tree dwarfing
   b. to demonstrate how to make an omelet
   c. to show how to take an effective snapshot
   d. to report the results of a recent experiment

3. General purpose: to persuade
   Specific purposes:

   a. to motivate my audience to contribute to CARE
   b. to prove to my audience that my new plan for ending the arms race will work
   c. to increase my audience's reverence for our flag
   d. to modify my audience's attitude about socialized medicine

Note that the specific purposes are phrases that begin with the infinitive form of a verb which clearly relates to one of the three general purposes of speech. Thus, speeches to entertain amuse, fascinate, amaze, delight; speeches to inform explain, make clear, demonstrate, report; and speeches to persuade motivate, prove, increase, modify.

The Central Idea

Once you have phrased your specific purpose statement, it is time to develop your central idea. The central idea may be thought of as the thesis, the key statement, or the controlling idea of the speech. Although it is related to the speech purpose, it is worded differently. A specific purpose statement is worded as an infinitive phrase. A central idea is worded as a complete sentence. The specific purpose statement always includes the infinitive form of the verb that clarifies what your purpose is, that is, to persuade, to inform, or to entertain. The central idea statement is a digested version of what you will be talking about in your speech. It is a one-sentence statement around which the entire speech is developed. The following guidelines will help you in developing your central idea statement.

The Central Idea Should Be a Complete Sentence

In most cases, a central idea should be stated as a simple complete sentence. Phrases, questions, or compound and complex sentences are usually not appropriate for central ideas.

Good: Being a single parent is tough.
(Simple, declarative sentence)

Bad: Are single parents getting a bad rap?
(Question)

Bad: Single parent problems
(Phrase)

Bad: After I raised Alex, I discovered being a single parent is tough.
(Complex sentence)

The Central Idea Should Be a Statement
You Must Explain or Defend

Your central idea should be a statement that requires clarification or reinforcement. Once you have developed your central idea, your next step will be to choose main points to support it. Following that you will choose supporting points to support the main points and so on. Therefore, you must develop your central idea with thoughtfulness and care so that the supports that you use will seem clear and logical to your audience.

In some cases, your central idea will break up quite naturally into three or four main points or logical divisions. For example, consider a speech with the central idea, Walking is the ideal exercise. You might support it with these three main points: (1) it can be done by almost anyone at any age, (2) it conditions the mind and body, and (3) it removes unwanted fat. In other cases, the main points supporting your central idea might be a series of steps like the four steps involved in making lasagna, the three steps in refinishing furniture and so on. Perhaps the main points supporting your central idea will be the reasons you give to convince your audience that your central idea is true.

The Central Idea Should Be Specific

State the central idea in specific rather than general terms. When you give your audience terms that are instantly understandable to them at the outset of your speech, they will be able to follow you more easily, and you won't have to waste their time defining terms for them as you unfold your ideas.

Vague: The U.S. Social Security System is in crisis.
Specific: The five-step Ball Plan can save Social Security.

The Central Idea Should Cover a Single Topic

Combining more than one topic in a speech will create frustration and confusion for both the speaker and the audience.

Bad: Unless we stop the influx of drugs into this country and stiffen the penalties for using and dealing, drug use by our youth will double in the next five years.

Good: There are three steps that must be taken to stop the influx of drugs into this country.

The Central Idea Should Be Audience Centered

Since you developed your subject and purpose with your audience in mind, you must show them that you considered them carefully when phrasing your central idea statement.

Good: Walking is the ideal exercise.
            (Includes practically everyone)

Bad: Walking is a good way to shed those extra pounds.
(Not everyone is overweight and someone who is might resent the comment.)

The Central Idea Should Relate to Purpose

Stating the central idea as a complete sentence will help you plan your communication more effectively. Following are three central idea statements related to three of the specific purpose statements.

Specific purpose—to amuse my audience by telling them how to wash a bull elephant.

Central idea—Washing a bull elephant isn't all that easy.

Specific purpose—to explain the art of tree dwarfing.

Central idea—The secret of tree dwarfing is twofold: cutting the root and branch system properly and maintaining the tree correctly.

Specific purpose—to motivate my audience to contribute to CARE.

Central idea—CARE is the most efficient and effective charity in the world.

As you can see, the central idea statement is a clear statement of the way in which you plan to develop your speech. For example, the first purpose above is to entertain, specifically to amuse the audience by telling them how to wash a bull elephant. The central idea—Washing a bull elephant isn't all that easy—implies that the speech will involve some of the humorous problems that could arise when trying to wash the elephant. The second purpose—to explain the art of tree dwarfing—is to inform. Its central idea indicates that the speech will deal with the two most important principles in tree dwarfing: cutting the roots and branches properly and maintaining the tree correctly. The third specific purpose—to motivate my audience to contribute to CARE—is to actuate. The central idea clearly indicates that you will develop the speech by talking about the efficiency and effectiveness of CARE.

Exercises

State whether the primary purpose in each of the following situations is (a) to inform, (b) to entertain, (c) to convince, (d) to reinforce, or (e) to actuate. Be prepared to explain and defend your answer.

1. The reading of a will
2. A TV shampoo commercial

3. A newscast
4. A debate
5. A eulogy at a funeral
6. An ornithology lecture
7. A TV soap opera
8. A campaign speech

Write a central idea statement and specific purpose statement for any of the following subjects as your instructor directs.

1. Alcoholism
2. Study habits
3. Crime
4. Listening
5. Education
6. Hobbies

3

Audience Analysis

After you have selected a subject and determined your purpose, you are ready to think of the speech in terms of your audience. An audience is an indispensable part of communication. If your audience fails to understand or pay attention to your message, communication does not take place. Therefore, when you develop your speech, do so with your audience in mind.

A speech that is prepared with a specific audience in mind is one that is audience centered. To aid in preparing an audience-centered speech, ask yourself the questions discussed in this chapter.

Who Exactly Is My Audience?

As you prepare the content of your speech, consider who is in your audience. Your boss or teacher? Your coworkers or classmates? Even if there is only one male or one female in an otherwise all-female or all-male audience, you must consider this person when preparing your speech. A surprising number of communications fail because the sender has been unclear as to the composition of his or her audience.

Take the case of George Scott, assistant cashier of a small midwestern bank. George came home in a state of dejection one night after having been passed over for promotion for the third time. He called his sister-in-law Phyllis, a close friend of the bank president's wife, and asked her to try to find out why. She learned the following: George considered himself a great storyteller and was particularly fond of ethnic jokes. He often told these jokes, both at the office and at holiday and other office get-togethers. What George failed to realize was that a number of people, including the bank president, found this sort of humor at the expense of others patently offensive. Whenever an opportunity for advancement occurred, George was rejected as being too insensitive. He paid a high price for not knowing his audience.

Consider your audience carefully, make note of their interests, consider their backgrounds, knowledge, and attitudes toward your subject, and then develop your speech accordingly.

What Response Can I Reasonably Expect from My Audience?

No matter how good a speech looks on paper or how well it is delivered, its success or failure must always be measured in terms of audience response. A salesperson who doesn't sell the product will soon be out of a job, the comedienne who doesn't evoke laughter will fall flat on her face, and the politician who doesn't get votes will not get elected. Therefore, when developing your speech, you must always consider your purpose in terms of audience response.

Some responses might be unattainable. Your audience might not have the background or experience necessary for you to be able to teach them how to repair a computer or sew a dress. A lack of time or resources might prevent you from showing your audience how to give a permanent or tile a floor. Your audience's attitude might be so opposed to your subject that they reject it at the outset. An example of the last would be trying to promote the legalization of marijuana in the United States. While some in your audience would be for it, others would be impossible to approach. In such cases you would be better off choosing another, more realistic purpose that could achieve a reasonable response.

Will My Audience Find This Subject Useful?

People willingly pay attention if they will gain something from doing so. You pay attention to the directions for filling out your income tax forms because you have something to gain if you do—and something to lose if you don't. You listen to a dull story told by your boss or prospective in-law and laugh because it is in your best interest to do so.

If for some reason members of your audience *need* to know the information you will be giving them in your speech, tell them they do. If they will prevent possible costly repair to their cars by engaging in a do-it-yourself lubricating program, if they have a responsibility to act against the growing problem of child abuse, or if they might possibly save a life by taking a Red Cross CPR course, let them know at the beginning of the speech. To show an audience how to react to an accident in the home and then explain to them only at the conclusion of your speech that the majority of accidents occur in the home would be to leave a number of those in your audience thinking, "I guess I should have listened."

Whenever possible, give your listener a reason for listening, and do it during the introduction to your speech.

Will My Audience Find This Subject Interesting?

The second reason that people pay attention is to satisfy an interest. Less effort is required to pay attention to what is interesting than to what is useful. Consider your own experience. Have you ever watched an unimaginative educational film because you knew there would be an exam about it? Have you listened to an uninteresting lecture because you knew it would have an effect on your grade? How much did you learn in that course? How much do you remember? In both cases you had, in effect, something to gain by paying attention. Did it pay off? Now compare the uninteresting educational film or the lecture to the educational TV program *Sesame Street*. It is estimated that *Sesame Street* has a viewing audience of ten million. The people who write and produce the program handle their material in such an interesting way that paying attention (and thus learning) is no longer a chore—it is fun. Your job as a speaker is to develop your material interestingly. While you can do this with someone you know quite well, how can you do it with strangers?

If you are familiar with the subject you have chosen, you should be able to make an educated guess.

Suppose you choose to speak about one of your two hobbies, raising tropical fish or restoring antique cars. The majority of your friends have shown more interest in your antique cars than in your fish. Some might have even changed the subject when you asked if they wanted to see your baby swordtails. Probably, a general audience would have greater initial interest in antique cars. This, however, does not mean you could not choose to speak about raising tropical fish. You can do it effectively if you build your audience's interest to gain and maintain their attention. You might begin by introducing your listeners to the piranha, one of the most interesting fish you own. A description of this voracious, sometimes man-eating creature as even more dangerous than the great white shark is a surefire attention getter.

What Is My Audience's Knowledge of My Subject?

Considering what your listeners already know about your subject is an important part of audience analysis. A too-technical approach could leave them thoroughly confused; repeating what they already know is sure to bore them.

If your audience has little or no knowledge of your subject, you must explain unfamiliar terminology and concepts to them. Keep in mind that this lack of knowledge will have an effect on their ability to respond. You could not expect those in your audience who have little idea of what is under the hood of a car to learn how to adjust a set of points or time a car after your speech to demonstrate. Nor could the nonsewer be expected to know how to install a zipper or cuff a pair of pants after a speech to demonstrate. Your educated guess as to the audience's knowledge of your subject should be an important consideration in terms of your choice of subject and purpose for each speech you make.

What Demographic Characteristics Should I Consider about My Audience?

The word *demography* is derived from the Greek word *demos,* meaning "people." The demographic consideration of your audience has to do with their vital statistics: age, education, beliefs, special interests, and so on. These characteristics can often help you in determining how to handle your subject. For example, as a rule, young people tend to be more physically active than older people, more inclined to engage in sports rather than watch them. Consequently, when talking about a particular sport, you might treat it as a participation sport for a younger audience and as a spectator sport for an older group.

The educational level of your audience could be important to you for a number of reasons. One of these has to do with the relationship between education and vocabulary. You must speak to an audience in familiar words that they can understand instantly. For example, you wouldn't explain the process of osmosis to your eleven-year-old sister in the same way you'd explain it to your college speech class. Another consideration is that a well-educated audience will be more aware of vital issues and current events than a less educated one will.

How many members of your audience come from different cultures? Never before in our history has the ethnic, cultural, and racial population in our country been so diverse. Each of us belongs to a variety of groups that have a distinct effect on the way we communicate. As indicated in Chapter 1, communication breakdowns occur even when communicating with those who are members of the groups to which we belong. Even more common are communication breakdowns between people from different cultures and subcultures. In analyzing your audience, try to consider any cultural characteristic, attitude, or sentiment that might bear on your speech topic.

Do those in your audience have similar attitudes and beliefs? Do they have special interests in common? Are they rich or poor, Democrat or Republican, conservative or liberal? Any of these demographic characteristics might be important to you as you prepare your speech. Remember, the success of your speech is always determined in terms of audience response. Did your audience get the information you wanted them to have? Were they entertained? Did you get them to take the action you wanted? The more you know about your audience, the more likely it will be that you will achieve your purpose.

Is My Audience's Attitude Favorable, Indifferent, or Opposed?

A Favorable Audience

Perhaps the greatest advantage to dealing with a favorable audience is that they are usually both supportive and attentive. Your goal when communicating to them is to reinforce their positive attitudes. If they enjoy humor, the more effectively you entertain them with your humor, the more successful you will be. If they would benefit from some tips on simple car maintenance, their satisfaction will be measured by how clearly you can explain your directions. The more effectively you can reinforce their positive attitudes, the more likely you will be to move them to action.

An Indifferent Audience

When an audience is indifferent, your job is to stimulate their interest. This can best be done by explaining the usefulness of the subject to them, by gaining their attention with a fresh imaginative approach, or by a combination of both. Take this action as soon as possible in your introduction. The sooner you can get the audience on your side, the better.

A successful speech to an indifferent audience was given by Erik Jackson, a second-year photography student. From conversations he had with them, Erik was aware that many of his classmates did not share his interest in photography and did not own expensive cameras or equipment. So, rather than delivering a complicated speech involving f-stops or light meters, Erik decided to give his speech class information about photography that would be useful to them no matter what kind of equipment they had.

Erik began his speech by showing those in his audience several pages of pictures from a photo album. He had enlarged each of the pictures so that they could easily be seen, even by those in the back of the room. He called his classmates' attention to the fact that other than there being different people in each, the photos were very much alike. In each snapshot people stood rigidly together in a line with smiles on their faces.

Next Erik showed the class a few variations of the first pictures he had shown. Although the people in them were the same, these snapshots were much more interesting than the first set. In some the arrangement of people was much more imaginative. In others the background made the group stand out much more vividly. By explaining about camera angle, posing, and picture balance, Erik demonstrated to his audience that with a little imagination they could take pictures that were more interesting.

An Opposed Audience

The hardest audience to deal with is one that includes many who disagree with your point of view or your subject. If you find that this is the case and you have a choice in the matter, you might consider choosing another topic. If you have no alternative, however, or are enthusiastic about your subject, concentrate on presenting your material so that you provide information that will make your audience less opposed toward your subject than they were when you started. Be aware that there is little change in viewpoint among those who listen to things with which they strongly disagree. Two useful suggestions for dealing with audiences opposed to a topic are (1) to establish a common ground with your audience, and (2) to provide them with information that will help to clear up any lack of understanding or misinformation they might have. Consider the following example:

Betty White, a college sophomore, decided to deliver a speech on one of her favorite subjects, opera. In talking to her classmates, she found that many in her audience were "turned off" by her topic. One student named Jeff even told her that he intended to cut class on the day of her speech because opera, especially Wagnerian opera, Betty's favorite, made him sick.

On the day of her speech Betty identified with many in her audience by beginning:

> *Four years ago I never would have dreamed of delivering a speech about opera to anyone. But then I found out an interesting fact. I didn't like opera because I did not know anything about it. Since then, the more I learn about*

opera the more I like it. And my guess is that when you get to know enough about it, you'll like it too.

Betty realized that if she was going to reach those in her audience who were opposed to her subject, she would have to identify with them and turn them on to the good things about opera with a fresh, imaginative approach. She prepared carefully and thoughtfully and delivered a humorous plot summary of Wagner's opera *Tannhauser,* which ended, to even Jeff's delight, with the heroine getting stabbed right between the two big trees.

Betty took what many in her audience thought would be a boring topic and made it exciting and interesting. She used humor, novelty, conflict, and suspense to hold their attention. The result was a successful speech.

In order to communicate successfully to an audience you must first understand them. Put yourself in their shoes. If you do, you will be much more likely to achieve your purpose. If you don't, you are liable to end up speaking to yourself and only a few others.

Exercises

1. Analyze five different magazines to determine the kinds of audiences to which they appeal.
2. Prepare a list of topics that would be interesting to your audience.
3. Prepare a list of topics that would be useful to your audience.
4. Analyze your class as an audience. In what ways are they similar? In what ways do they differ?
5. Pick a highly controversial issue such as abortion. Write a statement that favors or opposes it. Estimate how many in your class would agree with your statement, be indifferent to it, or oppose it. Survey the class to check your answer.
6. Analyze a popular TV show. To what age group is it directed? To what intelligence level would it appeal? Describe the characteristics of a "typical" viewer.
7. The audience analysis form (Figure 3-1) and the audience analysis evaluation form (Figure 3-2) are designed to aid you in better understanding your audience. Fill out a copy of the audience analysis form during the planning of your speech. Many of the answers you put down on the form will be educated guesses about your audience.

   Have your classmates fill out the audience analysis evaluation form to give you feedback as to how successful you were in analyzing and adapting to your audience.

AUDIENCE ANALYSIS FORM

Name _____ Date _____

Title of Speech _____

(Answer each question completely.)

THE COMMUNICATOR

1. Why have I chosen this subject?

2. What qualifies me to deal with this subject?

THE MESSAGE

3. What is my specific purpose?

4. What response can I reasonably expect?

THE AUDIENCE

5. Who is my audience?

6. Will my audience find this subject interesting?

7. Will my audience find this subject useful?

8. What is the audience's probable knowledge of my subject?

9. What characteristics of my audience should I consider in preparing my subject?

10. Is my audience's attitude toward this subject favorable, indifferent, or opposed?

FIGURE 3-1 Audience Analysis Form

AUDIENCE ANALYSIS EVALUATION FORM

Name _____

1. What was the communicator's subject?

2. How interesting was this subject to you?

    | | | | | |
    low   high

3. How useful was this subject to you?

    | | | | | |
    low   high

4. How effectively did the communicator get attention during introduction?

    | | | | | |
    low   high

5. How much preparation was put into this communication?

    | | | | | |
    low   high

6. What was the communicator's specific purpose? (one simple,
   declarative sentence)

    | | | | | |
    low   high

7. How effective was the conclusion to the communication?

    | | | | | |
    low   high

8. How well did the communicator accomplish his purpose?

    | | | | | |
    low   high

COMMENTS:

FIGURE 3-2   **Audience Analysis Evaluation Form**

4

Supporting Your Ideas

One of the best ways to improve your effectiveness as a speaker is to learn how to select and use supporting materials. Supporting materials are necessary to make your ideas clear or persuasive to your listener. Although there are different lists of supporting materials, most experts in the speech field agree on these six: examples, explanation, statistics, testimony, comparison/contrast, and visual aids. You have most likely used each of these during your lifetime, perhaps without being aware that there was a specific name for each. Suppose, for example, that you want to convince your parents that your new boyfriend is the ideal male. You might use any of the six supporting devices to support your assertion:

> Example: *"Mom and Dad, you're going to love Chris. He's one of the kindest people I've ever met. He puts in eight hours of volunteer work a week at the Mayville Nursing Home, he's a big brother to an eleven-year-old boy from the inner city, and he supports a little Cambodian child through the Christian Children's Fund."*
>
> Explanation: *"I see Chris as the perfect male. The consideration with which he treats me makes me feel special and loved, and his sensitivity to music, art, literature, and nature makes him a fascinating person to be with."*
>
> Statistics: *"Chris is six feet tall, he weights 180 pounds, and he makes over thirty thousand dollars a year."*
>
> Testimony: *"Rabbi Silberg, who is on the board of directors of Mayville Nursing Home, says Chris is one of the hardest working and best liked volunteers they have."*
>
> Comparison/Contrast: *"Chris isn't like any man I've ever met. The others have been interested in doing only what they want and in satisfying*

their own egos. Chris believes that love is a sharing, and that's the way he acts."

Visual Aids: *"Here are some snapshots of Chris. Doesn't he have a pleasant, open face? And did you notice how neatly he dresses?"*

Examples

When wisely chosen, the example is without a doubt the most effective and versatile of all the supporting devices. You would be wise to use at least one example as a support for every main point in your speech. An example is actually a typical sample selected to show the nature or character of the rest. Examples can be brief or detailed, factual or hypothetical, and humorous or serious. If an example is factual and familiar to your audience, you need only to cite it briefly since they know the details. If the example is hypothetical or unfamiliar to your audience, you must develop it in enough detail so that the point your story makes is clear to them. For instance, if you are talking about the problem of child abuse, and a highly publicized case has recently occurred in your community, you need only to mention the case briefly but clearly. If, however, the instance of abuse occurred in a different location or a number of years earlier, you might have to tell it as a short story with facts, names, and dates. Detailed examples are often called illustrations. These illustrations or stories can take the form of anecdotes, personal experiences, allegories, or parables. Using illustrations in your speech can provide your audience with clear mental pictures of particular instances or events.

When selecting supporting materials for your speech, look for appropriate and interesting examples that are clear, concise, and to the point. Note how the following examples support the speaker's central idea: Every adult American should have an up-to-date will.

Brief Factual Example

Although a will can be made out by an individual or for as little as twenty-five dollars by a lawyer, over 50 percent of all Americans die without ever having made one. No doubt many of them planned to, but just put it off. For example, Supreme Court Justice Fred Vinson died without a will, and Senator Robert Kerr was in the process of writing one when he died unexpectedly.

Brief Hypothetical Example

There are many reasons for keeping your will up to date. Suppose that you name your sister as executor, and she dies, moves away, or is too ill to serve? What if federal or state laws or court interpretations of them change? Suppose you move to a state where inheritance tax laws differ? All these are reasons for reviewing your will whenever major changes occur.

Detailed Factual Example

Uncle George died about a year ago. He had never made a will, and this created some real problems for his wife, Aunt Edna, and their three minor children. The checking and savings accounts were in my uncle's name and the bank wouldn't let Aunt Edna draw out any money. Because the deed for their house listed them as "tenants in common," the children were due to inherit two-thirds of the house. The result of this was that nobody would lend Aunt Edna money for a second mortgage on the house, and she could not sell it because as minors, the children couldn't "sign off" ownership in favor of their mother. The whole matter had to be taken to probate court, where it still is. To date, Aunt Edna has yet to see a single penny of Uncle George's estate and has borrowed over ten thousand dollars from her relatives.

Detailed Hypothetical Example

John Jones, a widower with four children, remarries. He registers everything he owns in joint ownership with the new Mrs. Jones knowing that she will provide for the children if he dies. A year later both are killed in an auto accident. To compound the tragedy, Mrs. Jones survives her husband by one hour, and his assets revert to her as co-owner. Unfortunately, Mrs. Jones had not made out a will, and the entire estate goes by law to her only blood relative, a cousin she doesn't even like. Because there was no will, none of Mr. Smith's assets went to his children, since Mrs. Smith was related to them only as a stepmother.

Explanation

The purpose of explanation is to make an idea clear or understandable. Obviously then, explanation qualifies as an excellent supporting device. Explanation can involve a number of different forms. It can include exposition, analysis, definition, and description.

A more comprehensive treatment of these supports is found on pp. 111–121.

Exposition

Exposition may be defined as communication that gives information to your listeners in order to increase their knowledge or their understanding of a situation or process. A speech on how to use a fly rod, bake a cake, lower a ceiling, or make a fortune in the stock market will in each case employ exposition. When a gas station attendant gives you directions on how to get to a nearby city, and you in turn pass his explanation on to the driver of the car you are traveling in, both conversations have largely involved exposition.

Analysis

Analysis is the process of explaining something by breaking it down into its parts and examining them. You use analysis when you explain how something works. If, for example, you want to convince your listeners to install inexpensive, homemade burglar alarm systems in their cars, you would have to give them a clear idea of what is involved in this system and how it would work. Another form of evaluation with which you are all familiar is the critique, or review. Perhaps you have attended a movie, play, or concert and afterwards totally disagreed with the review it received. Keep this in mind when you are using analysis as a supporting device so that you might do so as objectively as possible.

Definition

When you use a term or concept that is unfamiliar to your audience, you must define it either in your own words or in the words of someone else. Be careful not to use words in your definition that are more difficult to understand than the term or concept you are defining. For the sake of imaginativeness and interest, avoid using dictionary definitions. They are often overly formal and complex. Keep your definitions clear and to the point, using wording that your listeners can readily understand.

Description

Description makes use of the five sensory appeals (the five senses being taste, hearing, sight, touch, and smell) to make clear to your listener exactly what is being communicated. Although it isn't necessary to appeal to all five in each communication, the more of them to which you appeal, the more effective the communication. Effective description can create images or word pictures in the minds of your listeners.

Statistics

When used correctly, statistics can be an effective means of support. However, unless your statistics are both valid and reliable, they should not be used.

It was Benjamin Disraeli who said, "There are three kinds of lies: lies, damned lies, and statistics." His comment points up the fact that statistics can often be manipulated to support almost any assertion. For this reason it is wise to document the statistics you are using. This means indicating when and by whom the statistics were compiled. It is quite likely that there are those in your audience who have in the past been deceived by statistics. Put them at ease by using statistics that are up to date and compiled by a reputable source.

Try to make the statistics you use as interesting and uncomplicated as possible. Remember, it is your job as the speaker to maintain your listener's attention. Here are some suggestions to follow when using statistics.

Dramatize Your Statistics

If you can present your statistics in a dramatic or vivid way, they are more likely to be understood and remembered by your audience. When stated unimaginatively, statistics can often be quite dry. When stated in terms that a listener can visualize, they can be quite thought provoking. Consider this example from a student speech called "America's Disadvantaged Minority."

> *When we hear of the two hundred million children in the world who suffer from malnutrition or the fifty thousand children under the age of five who die each day from diarrhea, dehydration, or other preventable causes, or when we think of other young people in the world who are in peril, we usually think of those living in third world countries torn by either war or famine. Yet an October 8, 1990, article in* Time *magazine tells of America's most disadvantaged minority: its children. The article, written by Nancy Gibbs, reveals that nearly one-fourth of U.S. children under the age of six live in households struggling below the poverty level; that every eight seconds of the school day a child drops out; that every twenty-six seconds a child runs away from home; that every forty-seven seconds a child is abused; that every sixty-seven seconds an unwed teenager has a baby; that every seven minutes a child is busted for drug abuse; and that every thirty-six minutes one is killed or injured by a gun.*

Statistics presented in this manner are dramatic and easy to visualize, and therefore more likely to be remembered. To maintain credibility when presenting statistics as shocking as these, indicate the source of your information.

Round off Your Statistics

Remember, unless you repeat your statistics, your listeners will hear them only once. For this reason it is a good idea to round off complex numbers. Although it may be more exacting, instead of saying that the medium income of police officers in this city is $35,167, round it off to "around $35,000" or "slightly over $35,000." In the following excerpt the student-speaker rounds off the statistics she uses to support her proposition that in the mid 1990s racism is still rampant in America.

> *A recent survey of nearly fourteen hundred U.S. citizens by the National Opinion Research Center, a nonprofit group affiliated with the University of Chicago, found that 78 percent of the white respondents felt that blacks were more likely than whites to prefer welfare; that 62 percent felt blacks were more likely to be lazy; that 56 percent felt that blacks were more prone to violence; that 53 percent thought that blacks were less intelligent; and that 51 percent felt that blacks were less patriotic.*
>
> *Furthermore, even though more black Americans are getting college degrees these days, they still receive lower pay than white graduates for many jobs. Census figures released in September 1993 show the percentage of black men twenty-five and older with at least a bachelor's degree rose from 7.7 percent in 1980 to 11.9 percent in 1992. Among black women the rate rose from 8.1 percent to 12 percent. Nevertheless, the annual median salary for black college graduates was $30,910 compared to $37,490 for white college graduates.*

Display Your Statistics Visually

Complex statistical data should be presented on charts, tables, graphs, or diagrams in order to help your audience grasp what is being presented. A student used the example reproduced in Figure 4-1 (in a much larger form) to show that hypertension kills.

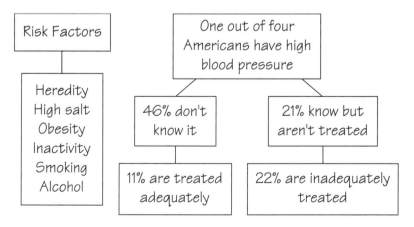

FIGURE 4-1   **Hypertension: The Silent Killer**

Testimony

We live in a complex age, an age of specialization. For this reason it is often wise for nonexpert speakers to support their ideas with the testimony of experts. The testimony of an expert or authority on a particular subject carries the weight of that person's education and experience. Few of us would quarrel with an opthalmologist who recommended that we switch to bifocals or an auto mechanic who told us that we needed a new vacuum advance. Unless we questioned their honesty or competency, we would have no reason to doubt their judgment. Consequently, when you are delivering a speech, support your opinions if need be with the opinions of others more expert than you to add credibility to your presentation.

When supporting your point of view with the testimony of others, you can either quote them verbatim or paraphrase what they have said in your own words. The decision is up to you. There are, however, two instances when it is better to quote directly than to paraphrase: (1) when the person you are quoting has said it so well you cannot possibly say it better, and (2) when the testimony is controversial and you want your audience to hear it straight from the source. Otherwise, it is perfectly acceptable to state the testimony in your own words. When doing so, be careful to paraphrase the testimony of another both fairly and accurately. As a speaker, you have a responsibility to be honest and straightforward.

If the experts you are citing are likely to be unfamiliar to those in your audience, give facts about them that will establish their credibility. Your listeners will give more heed to what Dr. Carl J. George, chairman of the department of psychology at the University of Wisconsin and author of *Knowing Your Child,* has to say about teenage suicide than they will to what Carl J. George or even Dr. Carl J. George has to say.

Although it is often important that the authority you are citing is up to date, this is not always necessary. It can often be very effective to back up your point of view by citing an authority from the past that most of your audience respects. For example, a reference to the Bible or other holy books can often be quite effective. These volumes contain a wealth of material on almost any subject of importance. Note how effectively Dr. Martin Luther King, Jr., challenges the conscience of America by citing those authorities who framed the Constitution and the Declaration of Independence:

> *When the architects of our Republic wrote the magnificent words of the Constitution and the Declaration of Independence, they were signing a promissory note to which every American was to fall heir. . . . It is obvious today that America has defaulted on this promissory note, insofar as her citizens of color are concerned. Instead of honoring this sacred obligation, America has given the Negro people a bad check; a check which has come*

back marked insufficient funds. However, we refuse to believe that there are insufficient funds in the great vaults of opportunity of this nation. And so we've come to cash this check, a check that will give us on demand the riches of freedom and the security of justice.

The use of testimony as a support is often less effective when dealing with a controversial subject. Anyone who has had anything to do with debate is aware that when you are dealing with a controversial subject of significance, there is sure to be an unlimited number of experts who disagree with one another.

Provided you have some expertise in regard to your subject, one of the best forms of testimony you can use is your own personal experience. If you have some background or experience in regard to your subject that qualifies you as somewhat of an expert, mention it in the introduction to your speech. Let your listeners know immediately that you are backing up the information you are giving them with your own "expert" testimony. If you wait until the middle or end of your speech to tell them about your background, chances are that some in your audience will think, "I didn't know the speaker was an expert on the subject. I guess I should have listened more carefully."

Comparison/Contrast

One of the basic principles of education is that the only way you can learn anything new is to be able to relate it to something you already know. Therefore, the best way to teach the unknown is to compare it to the known. Jesus used comparison very effectively when he preached to the different people he met. Depending upon the backgrounds and occupations of those in his audience at the time, he variously revealed what the kingdom of heaven is like by comparing it to: a fisherman throwing his net into the sea and pulling in both good fish and bad, a farmer harvesting his wheat along with weeds, a merchant selling all he had to buy a single pearl of great value, and ten bridesmaids who took their lamps and went to meet the bridegroom. This kind of comparison is called figurative comparison or analogy. It describes similarities between things that are otherwise different. Other examples are the comparison of a bargaining meeting to a barroom brawl and a major speech to a parachute jump without a parachute.

A literal comparison describes similarities between things that are physically alike. It can often give your listener a clear mental picture of what you are talking about. For instance, if you say that the new dean of men looks like a young Alec Baldwin or that a Trident submarine is half again as long as a football field, you are offering your listener a clear basis of comparison. Less visual examples would be comparisons between interest rates in the United

States in 1994 and 1995, academic standards in private and public universities, and jazz versus rhythm and blues. Literal comparisons are often used to reinforce particular points of view. How many times have you heard or used an argument similar to the following: "Why can't I learn to drive? Sally already has her driver's license, and she's a year younger than I am"?

Comparing differences is often called contrast. When you compare high school and college, living at home or living on your own, and apples and oranges, you are emphasizing differences rather than similarities between like things. Consider the comment, "Boy, you kids nowadays get away with murder. When I was your age I wouldn't dream of doing that." You are backing up your point of view by emphasizing differences rather than similarities.

Visual Aids

Often it is necessary to use visual aids when presenting your supporting material. Some material is almost impossible to present without using them. Try demonstrating how to use a slide rule without a slide rule or a facsimile of one. Try contrasting impressionism with surrealistic art without showing your audience examples of each. When used effectively, visual aids can be an effective means of reinforcing and clarifying your ideas. An audience will retain the information you give them longer if they are both told and shown something at the same time. The old adage, A picture is worth a thousand words, applies. Effectively used, audiovisual aids will enhance your audience's interest and understanding. Be mindful, however, that the aid should only reinforce or clarify your material. Showing your audience a good video, movie, or slide show would effectively hold their attention but would be an ineffective substitute for your speech. The word *aid* means to help or assist. That is what your visual aid should do. Some often-used visual aids are listed below.

    The item itself
    Charts, graphs, and diagrams
    Slides and filmstrips
    Transparencies for overhead projectors
    Flyers, pamphlets, and handouts
    Paintings and posters
    Chalkboards and flip charts
    Photographs and drawings
    CDs, audiotapes, and videotapes
    Records and movies
    Yourself or others
    Models and facsimiles
    Computer-generated materials

Benefits of Visual Aids

Visual aids help an audience remember what you say. An audience is far more likely to remember information when they are both told and shown something at the same time. For example, after seventy-two hours, most people can only remember 10 percent of what they have seen, 20 percent of what they have heard, but almost 65 percent of what they have both seen and heard.

Visual aids increase understanding. Models allow your audience to visualize things that are difficult to describe in words alone. Charts and graphs can make complex statistics and relationships easier for your audience to understand.

Visual aids add interest to your speech and help to hold the attention of your audience. When effectively chosen, visual aids provide creativeness and variety to your presentation. The use of color in your aids will help you get and hold attention.

Visual aids reduce the amount of time you would have to spend giving lengthy explanations. The use of slides, transparencies, and computer display panels are helpful when a subject is complex. If these are impractical or unavailable, consider using handouts. Handouts should be distributed before you begin speaking and explained early in the speech.

Visual aids can give your speech a polished, professional look. An LCD (liquid crystal display) panel allows you to display material from your computer through an overhead projector. A converter will allow you to display the material on a wide-screen TV. Although this technique requires considerable computer skill, the effect can be quite impressive. Imagine presenting complex statistics that can be changed as your viewers watch.

Specific Suggestions for Using Visual Aids

When used effectively, visual aids can be an excellent means of reinforcing or clarifying your ideas. If, however, the visual aid is used incorrectly, it can detract from rather than improve your speech. Here are some specific suggestions for using visual aids:

1. A visual aid must be large enough to be seen by the entire audience. If you are using a poster or chart, make sure that your lettering or drawings are dark or vivid enough so that those farthest away will get the information. Unless each member of your audience can see your visual aid clearly, don't use it.

2. Avoid visual aids that are overly complex. A complicated drawing or too many words or statistics will defeat your purpose. A listener must be able to grasp the meaning of your visual instantly.

3. Your visual aid should clarify or reinforce your point. Displaying a picture of yourself holding a string of bass during a demonstration on how to fillet fish might do something for your ego but will add nothing to your audience's understanding.

4. Make sure that you maintain good eye contact when referring to your visual aid. It is for the audience, not you, to look at. Besides, looking out at your audience will help you determine if you are displaying your visual aid in a way that can easily be seen by all.

5. Whenever possible, use posterboard or a flip chart rather than a chalkboard during your presentation. If you must use a chalkboard, avoid turning your back to the audience for an extended period. Limit your use of the board to a simple drawing or a few words or phrases, or put what you need on the board before you begin the speech.

6. Keep your visual aid out of sight except when you are using it. Attention is intermittent. A person pays attention to something for a while, stops for a moment or so, and goes back to paying attention again. If you leave an interesting visual aid out to look at, chances are that some in your audience might find themselves paying attention to it rather than your speech.

7. Include your visual aid when practicing your speech. Become so familiar with your visual aid that you can refer to any part of it with little loss of eye contact. Know where your aids will be when you want them and where you will put them when they are not being used.

8. Never pass a visual aid around through the audience. If you do, you will lose the attention of at least three listeners—the one looking at the aid, the one who has just passed it on, and the one who will be getting it next. An exception would be if you were passing out an aid or handout to each member of your audience. There is less chance that this activity will be distracting if you pass the items out near the end of your speech, perhaps even at the conclusion.

9. Make sure that your visual aid does not take up too much time. Remember, you are using the visual aid to support a point you are making in your speech, not as a section of the speech itself. Running three minutes of a movie or slides during a five-minute speech is an overly long and inappropriate use of visual aids. On the other hand, make sure that everyone has enough time to see and understand your visual aid.

10. Do not let your visual aid interfere with the continuity of your speech. If, for example, you are going through the steps of mixing the ingredients of a cake or applying glaze to a ceramic during a speech to demonstrate, don't stop talking to your audience while doing so. Your visual aid must support what you are saying, not substitute for it.

11. Be prepared to deliver your speech without your visual aid. No matter how careful you are when preparing and practicing with your visual aid, something can go wrong. Slide projectors can break, CDs or cassette players can malfunction, and markers or chalk can mysteriously disappear. Knowing that you can deliver your speech even if your visual aid fails will give you a sense of confidence and allow you to be more relaxed. Keep in mind, furthermore, that the ability to deliver a speech effectively when your visual aid fails will win you the admiration and respect of your audience.

12. Avoid presenting too much material on a visual aid. An overly complex visual aid may be worse than none at all. A visual aid should be clear, concise, and instantly intelligible.

Combined Supports

Often, supporting materials are used in combination with one another. Thus you might support a point of view with comparative statistics, a visual aid that has to be explained, an example that includes expert testimony, and so on. Tests, experiments, studies, surveys, polls, programs, and investigations often involve a combination of supporting devices. For example, the benefits of an exercise program might be stated in terms of comparison, testimony, and statistics. An investigation into the effects of budget cuts on the poor might involve examples, testimony, comparison, and statistics. Either subject might be explained to an audience with the help of a visual aid.

Exercises

1. Choose one of the following statements or write one of your own and support it with examples, explanation, statistics, testimony, and comparison/contrast.

   "Gambling should be legalized in the United States."
   "The United States should pass a law abolishing the death penalty."
   "The United States should restore friendly relations with Cuba."

2. Indicate an authority your classmates would respect in the following fields: science, education, energy, medicine, law, football, baseball, and music.
3. Find an ad that combines two or more supporting devices to sell its products. Do the supporting devices seem accurate and objective? Comment on whether you think the ad is effective and why or why not.

5

Gathering Supportive Material

Chapter 2 suggests that you choose a subject that suits the purpose of your speech and that is interesting to you. This is wise because if you are going to be collecting facts and gathering ideas for your speech, you will be spending some time on it. Start collecting information on your subject immediately and try to examine as wide a variety of resources as possible.

You can gather information for your speech in a number of ways: (1) develop it from your own knowledge and experience, (2) access it from written sources primarily through a library, (3) gather it through electronic resources, (4) acquire it through interviews, and (5) write to organizations or individuals who have specialized information about your topic.

Personal Experience and Knowledge

If the subject you have chosen is from your own experience or knowledge, then this is the first place to start when gathering supporting material for your speech. Keep in mind that your experiences include not only your personal involvement with, or observation of, events as they occurred but also those things you have experienced vicariously by reading or hearing about them. There are a number of ways to use personal experience when planning your speech. First, you can develop a speech to entertain in which you tell a story about something exciting, suspenseful, fascinating, unusual, or humorous that has happened to you.

Second, you can develop a persuasive speech to make a point in which you tell your audience about an experience you had that taught you a lesson.

In the speech of personal experience to make a point there are two possible approaches: (1) the main idea (the point) is stated at the beginning of the speech followed by a story that reinforces it, and (2) the story is told first, and the point is made at the conclusion of the speech. Thus, you might say, "I learned at an early age never to trust strangers," and tell your audience about an experience you had that taught you this lesson, or you might relate the experience first and end by saying, "and that's how I learned never to trust strangers."

Finally, you can use your own experience and knowledge to compile a list of ideas on a particular topic. If your own knowledge or experience qualifies you as somewhat of an expert in a particular area you might be the only resource needed to develop your speech. Even if you are not an expert, you may be amazed at the amount of information you can come up with when brainstorming a topic with which you are familiar. If your list of ideas comes entirely from your own knowledge or experience, you might be able to develop your speech without doing any further research. In most cases, however, you will have to do some research to add to the materials you already have. Keep in mind that you may choose to do your speech on a topic you find interesting but know little about. In this case, before brainstorming, you will want to do preliminary research not only to gather ideas but also to determine if there is sufficient material available to develop an effective speech on that topic.

Brainstorming

Brainstorming is an excellent technique for generating ideas on your subject. The principle is to come up with as many ideas as possible about your topic as fast as you can think of them. Write them all down. Pay no attention to their quality and don't evaluate them. Don't worry if some seem irrelevant; you can discard them later. After you have listed as many ideas as you can, you are ready for step two: Clustering.

Clustering

In step two, you put your topic down and write down all the ideas you have come up with on your brainstorming list that relate to it. Analyze the list carefully. See if you can identify any ideas as main points, supporting points, or subpoints for your speech. Use arrows to indicate their relationship to each other as shown in Figure 5-1.

The cluster of words around the topic "our cafeteria" reflects your concepts of the cafeteria. You see the cafeteria as being clean, convenient, inexpensive, a good place to meet people, and so on. Keep in mind that as you develop the cluster into a framework for your speech, not everything will be

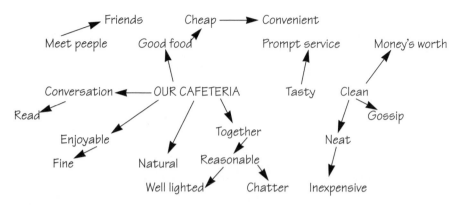

FIGURE 5-1   Clustering

used. Some things will be left out and others may be changed. The important thing is that you have begun to gather ideas for your speech. Now you can consider ways to locate material other than through your own knowledge and experience. Consider interviewing people who work at the cafeteria. How about the managers? The buyers? Someone in the business office who is familiar with cafeteria records? Do some of your classmates or friends frequent the cafeteria? Has the school newspaper done an article on the cafeteria recently? The answers to these questions might contribute to a useful and interesting speech for your audience.

The Library

A well-equipped library is the best place to find written information for your speech. A newspaper is an excellent source of up-to-date information. A good library will have the latest editions of local, national, and international newspapers as well as recent back copies or microfilm. Some newspapers have indexes which list by subject the articles that have appeared in that paper. *The New York Times Index* lists subject, date, page, and column of every article that has appeared in that paper since 1913.

In the library reference room you will find almanacs, atlases, biographies, encyclopedias, and countless other reference books filled with pertinent information on almost any topic. Usually located on open shelves, these books are labeled with an "R" for reference. Because they are meant for research, they must be used on the premises and cannot be checked out. If you need help finding appropriate reference volumes, consult *Winchell's Guide to Reference Books* or ask the reference librarian for assistance.

One of the best sources for information for your speech is *The Readers' Guide to Periodical Literature.* Updated ten times each year, it indexes information found in 177 popular magazines such as *The Atlantic, Ebony, Esquire, Harper's, National Geographic, Popular Science, Rolling Stone, Sports Illustrated,* and *Vital Speeches of the Day. Readers' Guide* lists articles alphabetically by subject headings or author's last name to make research simpler and quicker. Once you have found the articles you need, write down the information in the entry on an index card. Include the title of the article, the author, the name of the magazine, the volume number, the page number, and the issue date.

When you have the necessary information, you are ready to locate the magazine. Magazines are located alphabetically by title or on a periodical holding list. Current issues are located in the periodical section. If you have trouble locating a magazine, ask a librarian.

The Computerized Catalog

A computerized catalog makes it easy to find the library materials you want because the program prompts you step-by-step. Even if you only know part of a subject title or author's name, keyword searching will look for all occurrences of that word or words anywhere in the library's listing of materials.

Electronic Services

Computerized Research Services

Library computerized research services have expanded greatly in the last few years. Many libraries feature computerized card catalogs and have the ability to access the card catalogs of neighboring libraries. Some offer those who have computers equipped with modems and telephone hookups the opportunity to access their catalog and research services from home or office practically twenty-four hours a day. As of 1994, DIALOG, the world's largest on-line databank of information, has grown to over four hundred databases, which cover practically any topic imaginable from aardvarks to zygotes. Because of their popularity and usefulness, computerized research services are constantly improving. New programs are being developed and existing programs are continually being updated and expanded.

Since these services are expensive, many libraries try to avoid duplicating one provided by another library in the same area. Consequently, if you fail to find a specific program in your school or local library, check the computer centers of neighboring libraries, particularly university, college, or well-equipped high school libraries in your area. Ask them if they provide the services listed as follows or any that are similar.

Database Services

ProQuest
This service is a computerized index of more than nine hundred magazines, which is five times as many periodicals as is listed in *The Readers' Guide to Periodical Literature*. ProQuest is a full-image product, which means the entire magazine, including pictures, can be accessed.

SIRS (Social Issues Resource Services)
SIRS is a full-text CD-ROM program that includes thousands of articles related to social issues, science developments and issues, global events, and issues of historic, economic, or political importance.

STATBANK
STATBANK is a comprehensive resource of key facts and figures on every state in the United States and more than two hundred foreign countries. It includes the latest information plus historical data on everything from the AIDS problem in the United States to the estimated number of tons of cocaine entering this country from Peru.

CD NEWSBANK
This full-text CD-ROM information service provides complete articles from major newspapers throughout the United States and Canada as well as verbatim news stories from national and international wire services. It covers such diverse topics as health, science, social issues, the environment, and internal affairs.

You don't have to be an expert to take advantage of these computer programs. Many of them provide a search format designed for first-time users. If the program you choose does not have a search format, ask the reference librarian for assistance.

OCLC, Inc.
OCLC, Inc. is a national bibliography database with over fifteen million bibliographic records serving over 6,000 participating institutions throughout the world.

Newspaper Abstracts Ondisc
Newspaper Abstracts Ondisc provides rapid access to nine major U.S. newspapers. It lists more than 1,222,000 records from 1985 to present and provides rapid access to news-oriented information.

Foreign Broadcast Information Service
Foreign Broadcast Information Service covers translated materials from foreign radio and TV broadcasts plus newspaper and periodical articles.

Business Newsbank
Business Newsbank covers business-related articles in more than six hundred resources.

Academic Search (EBSCOhost)
Academic Search (EBSCOhost) provides abstracts and citations to nearly 3,000 newspapers, magazines, and journals with complete articles available from 1,000 of these titles.

CARL Uncover
CARL Uncover is a database of major articles from over 17,000 journals, updated daily.

MEDLINE
MEDLINE is a bibliographic database of the National Library of Medicine containing complete references to articles from more than 3,200 biomedical journals.

The Internet

In the last decade, academic research has been improved significantly by the Internet, an immense and complex international communication system made up of millions of computers from all over the world. The Internet provides the latest information from publications, educational institutions, and information centers worldwide. Over the years programs have been developed for communicating and exchanging information over the Internet. In order to use the Internet on your own personal computer, you need to have a computer software package, a modem connected to your computer and your phone, and and a commercial server such as America Online or Microsoft Network. These servers charge varying fees. However, most colleges and universities offer Internet access to their students and faculty free of charge. Internet offerings and databases continue to grow at a phenomenal rate. One of the disadvantages of the Internet is that many new users find its vastness overwhelming. You can follow information according to your research needs. However, because many links are not straightforward and you don't know where the link will take you, getting lost is a distinct possibility. You will need to allow yourself time to explore the Internet to become familiar with what it has to offer. The Internet allows users to search for information on the World Wide Web, exchange both national and international e-mail, and participate in "newsgroups"—a worldwide public facility for debate and the open exchange of information.

The World Wide Web

The Internet's newest and easiest tool for accessing information is the World Wide Web. The Web projects information on easy-to-read screens, or "pages." On the Web page you can click a graphic or an underlined name, fact, or concept that you want to know more about and your click takes you to another Web page with information about that subject. You use a program called a *browser* to navigate through the Web. There are millions of Web pages. Their topics range from the complete works of Mozart to recent infant mortality rates in Third-World countries. Since there are no rules to prevent those who create Web pages from making whatever links they choose, it is easy to get sidetracked on the Web. For example, clicking Hans Christian Andersen on a page about writers might lead you to a page about Andersen's birthplace, Odense, Denmark. The page is likely to produce links to articles about socialism, kringle, Danish sandwiches, Danish beer, and Copenhagen's Tivoli, the Danish amusement park that inspired Disneyland.

When searching for specific information on the Web, you can use one of the Web's search engines to access the information you need. The Webcrawler is a useful and easy-to-use search engine. It helps you find software and files quickly and easily. At times, it may take longer than you expect to connect to a Web site. Several factors can affect your connection time including the server you are using, how far away the site is, and how fast your modem is.

Electronic Mail

Electronic mail (or e-mail) is a fast and efficient way to send mail to others without having to use stationery, an envelope, or a stamp. Not only is e-mail a boon to students for educational purposes, but it allows them to keep in touch inexpensively with relatives and friends. If you know how to use a word processor, you can write an electronic letter.

Telnet

If you have your own personal computer with a modem and telephone hookup, or have access to one, you can use that computer as a terminal to link to your school's library. When you log onto a computer with Telnet software, your computer acts like a terminal. If your school library allows Telnet access to its computer, you can do at home what other students do on campus. Simply dial the library's phone number through your modem to access the Library Computer Catalog. In a typical university library the card catalog and other databases exist on-line. To find Telnet sites you must use an Internet search engine such as the Webcrawler. Once you connect to a Telnet site, you must use the commands for the software at that site. Some useful Telnet sites include:

United States Library of Congress
The Library of Congress lists nearly every book published in the United States. You can also gain access to other U.S. government services and other library databases.

Federal Information Exchange
The Federal Information Exchange offers information for women and minorities about opportunities, grants, and programs within U.S. government bureaus.

Washington University Library
This site offers access to research facilities and libraries around the world.

Usenet

Usenet is an interactive international magazine that covers a vast array of subjects in science and everyday life. Usenet consists of thousands of newsgroups. Each newsgroup is composed of a series of electronic articles on a particular topic. The topic can be anything from mud wrestling to voodoo to the latest news about AIDS research. In effect Usenet is Internet's open-discussion forum. Usenet allows you to take part in discussion with experts in a field you have an interest in.

Interviewing

An interview can be an effective and interesting way to gather information. Up-to-date information from an expert in the field can often carry a great deal of weight. Faculty members, clergy, community leaders, and local politicians are among those who would be pleased to provide you with speech material. Keep in mind, though, that no matter how expert the person you are interviewing is, you don't want to overload your speech with references to that interview. Unless you are an experienced note taker, you will want to tape-record your interview. Most subjects will gladly give you permission to tape-record them if you explain exactly how you want to use the material.

You can also interview people electronically over Usenet. Add to the credibility of your speech with a statement supporting your plea for higher emission standards from a world-renowned environmentalist. Support your call for National Health Insurance with statements from Norwegian citizens who have had socialized medicine in their country for more than eighty-eight years.

Writing away for Materials

If you begin your preparation early enough, you may have time to write away for information that could add to the effectiveness of your speech. Government agencies, private institutions, qualified experts, and special-interest groups will often provide free and useful information on a variety of topics. For example, when researching the topic sports drugs, you might write to organizations such as the ones below:

> National Institute of Drug Abuse
> Reason Foundation
> Hastings Center
> Office of National Drug Control Policy
> Institute for Social and Cultural Change

For a list of these and similar groups and their mailing addresses consult the *Encyclopedia of Associations* in your library's reference section. Writing away for information can often provide impressive and up-to-date data.

Bibliography Cards

As you gather the supporting materials for your speech, you should make one bibliography card for each source you use. Use standard three-by-five-, four-by-six-, or five-by-eight-inch index cards. If you choose to make your own cards rather than buy them, use rigid cardboard. For books, your card should include the name of the author, book title, publisher, place and date of publication, and call number. A bibliography card for a periodical should include the author, title of the article, magazine title, date of publication, and page number(s). Figure 5-2 shows a sample bibliography card for a periodical article, and Figure 5-3 shows a sample bibliography card for a book.

> J. Rubinstein, "Survival in the
> Night [needles exchange program
> triggers memories of being robbed
> in New York]"   The New Yorker
> v 69 pp. 74–8 August 23–30 '93

FIGURE 5-2   Sample Bibliography
Card—Periodical

```
┌─────────────────────────────────────┐
│  Koch, Arthur                        │
│            Speaking with a Purpose   │
│            4th ed.  Boston, MA.      │
│            Allyn and Bacon           │
│            1998                      │
│   651.2                              │
│   A692                              │
└─────────────────────────────────────┘
```

FIGURE 5-3   Sample Bibliography Card—Book

Taking Notes

The more accurate your notes are, the less time you will have to spend rechecking your sources for dates, statistics, and exact wording.

Although you can record your material in notebooks or loose-leaf folders, I find that the use of note cards is best. There are a number of reasons for this: (1) Note cards are easy to handle. If a note card contains information that you decide not to use, you can throw it away; (2) Note cards can be shuffled and used to organize the speech; (3) Note cards can easily be used for reference during the delivery of the speech or during the question-and-answer period following it; and (4) Note cards can more easily be grouped and classified. Here are some suggestions to follow when taking your notes:

1. Use uniform note cards. Whether you buy them or make them yourself, note cards that are uniform in size and stiffness are easier to work with and store.
2. Record the exact source of your information. When the source is written, indicate the call number, author(s), title, date, publisher, and page numbers in case you want to refer to the source again. If your information came from an interview, indicate the time and date of the interview along with the interviewed person's name and credentials.
3. Keep notes brief. Don't copy large selections of material at random. Be selective. Spend time deciding exactly what you want to say before writing.
4. Be accurate. If you are copying a direct quotation, make sure that the wording is exact. If you are paraphrasing, make sure the paraphrase accurately conveys the meaning of the original.
5. Indicate the subject of each note card. Then when you are ready to organize your speech, you can put the cards in piles according to the points they are supporting.

6. Take an ample number of notes. Don't be afraid of gathering too much information. It is much easier to select the best from an overabundance of information than to find you are short and have to go back and look for more.

Bibliography

It is sometimes necessary to include a bibliography with your speech outline to document the sources of your supporting material. A bibliography should be arranged alphabetically by the author's last name or the first important word in the title. When including a bibliography, type the first line flush with the left margin and indent subsequent lines. Use the samples below as models:

An Article in a Periodical
"Withdrawal symptoms." J. Weber Jr. *Business Week* pp. 20–1 Ag 2 '93
"Clues in the brain (role of messolimbic dopamine system in drug and alcohol addiction)." B. Came. Maclean's v106 pp. 40–1 Jl 19 '93

A Book
Koch, Arthur. *Speaking with a Purpose.* 4th ed. Boston, MA: Allyn and Bacon, 1998.

One advantage of using electronic resources when gathering supporting materials for your speech is that if you use a computer connected to a printer or access the information from your personal computer, you can record the information you need with the press of a button.

Exercises

1. Answer the following questions about your school library.

   a. What hours is your library open?
   b. What is the name of the person in charge?
   c. To which newspapers does your library subscribe?
   d. For what period of time can a book be checked out?
   e. What fines are imposed for overdue books or records?
   f. List the computerized services at your library.

6

Preparing the Content of Your Speech

Now that you have gathered the supporting materials you will need to reinforce or clarify your central idea and main points, you are ready to begin preparing the content of your speech. The content should be developed around the central idea statement, which is the controlling idea of the speech. With a basic speech pattern you might simply state and support the central idea. Speeches of personal experience to entertain or to make a point are often developed in this statement-support pattern.

In the speech of personal experience to make a point, there are two possible approaches: (1) the central idea (the point) is stated at the beginning of the speech followed by a story that reinforces it, and (2) the story is told first, and the point is made at the conclusion of the speech. Thus you might say, "I learned at an early age never to trust strangers," and tell your audience about an experience you had that taught you this lesson, or you might relate the experience first and end by saying, "And that's how I learned never to trust strangers."

In most cases, however, the central idea of a speech quite naturally breaks up into two or three main points. For example, consider a speech with the topic "Our Cafeteria"—the brainstorming example from Chapter 5. In developing the topic "Our Cafeteria," which was a clean, inexpensive, good place to meet people, and so on, you could quite likely come up with the central idea, "Our school cafeteria is an excellent place to eat." You might support it with these three main points: (1) the prices are reasonable, (2) the food is well prepared, and (3) the surroundings are neat and clean. The basic format for this speech would be as follows:

Introduction: *The introduction of a speech should capture the audience's attention, give them a reason for listening, present the central idea of the speech—in this case, Our school cafeteria is an excellent place to eat—indicate your qualifications for giving the speech, and preview the main points of the speech.*

Body: *First main point—the prices are reasonable (supporting material).*

Second main point—the food is well prepared (supporting material).

Third main point—the surroundings are neat and clean (supporting material).

Conclusion: *The conclusion of a speech should end with a summary, a restatement of the central idea, a question, a call to action, or a vision of the future.*

Although some central ideas can logically be broken down into five or more main points, it is advisable to limit your speech to no more than four. Keep in mind that you are speaking to listeners, who must assimilate and remember the information you are giving them. Few, if any, will be taking notes. If you have too many points, the chances are great that you will wind up confusing and perhaps even losing some of your audience.

Organizing Your Speech

As you can see from the format above, a speech is divided into three parts—the introduction, the body, and the conclusion. Each of these parts has a particular function.

Introduction

An introduction should capture the attention of the audience, give them a reason for listening, present the central idea, indicate your qualifications, and preview the main ideas to be given. As a rule of thumb, the introduction should comprise from 10 to 15 percent of the total speech time and should lead smoothly into the body of the speech.

Body

The body should comprise from 75 to 85 percent of the speech. That is where the speaker's message is presented. The body consists of the main points of the speech, along with the supporting materials necessary to develop each point, and clear transitions from each point to the next.

Conclusion

A conclusion should be short and to the point. It should comprise from 5 to 10 percent of the total speech and include one or any combination of the following: a summary of the main points, a restatement of the central idea, a question, a call to action, a vision of the future, and so on.

Planning the Body

The body is the most important part of the speech. It contains the development of the central idea, the major points, and the supporting material that proves or clarifies the central idea and main points. Therefore, it is wise to develop the body of the speech first. Follow these four steps as you plan the body of your speech:

1. Decide on the main points that will support or clarify your central idea.
2. Write these main points as complete sentences.
3. Arrange the central idea and main points in a logical organizational pattern.
4. Add appropriate supporting material to clarify and reinforce your central idea and main points.

Decide on Main Points

The central idea statement you have chosen should determine the main points you select. The number of main points you need to put your ideas across is up to you. In some speeches, as you remember, the body may consist simply of the support you are using for your central idea. In others you might choose two to four main points around which to build your speech. Keep in mind during this stage that you are trying to get your audience to accept and remember your ideas. As I pointed out earlier, if you develop any more than four main points, chances are that some of your audience will be unable to remember them.

Write Your Main Points as Complete Sentences

Writing your main points as complete sentences will help you determine whether they reinforce or clarify your central ideas effectively and whether they cover your subject adequately. Each main point should be stated clearly and succinctly so there is no doubt in your listeners' minds as to what your point is and what you are trying to accomplish. Following are four suggestions for developing main points for your speech:

1. They should clarify or reinforce your central idea.
2. They should cover your subject adequately.
3. They should be equal in importance.
4. They should be worded in a similar way.

They Should Clarify or Reinforce Your Central Idea

In order to be effective, your main points must make your central idea clearer or more forceful. These main points will in turn be clarified or reinforced by your supporting materials: examples, illustrations, statistics, explanation, testimony, comparison/contrast, and visual aids. Main points that do not clearly reinforce or clarify your central idea are confusing. Consider the following example:

> *Central idea:* Iguanas make great pets.
> *Main point:* They are inexpensive.
> *Main point:* They are clean.
> *Main point:* They are easy to care for.
> *Main point:* They are reptiles.

Note that while the first three main points reinforce the central idea that iguanas make great pets, the fourth point, that they are reptiles, does not. While it can be argued that many reptiles make excellent pets, most would agree that others, like cobras or crocodiles, do not.

They Should Cover Your Subject Adequately

In order to achieve your purpose in speaking, you must be sure to provide your listeners with the information they need to respond correctly. Choose your main points carefully so that they fully develop your central idea. It is always better to have too much material than to fail to cover a subject adequately. Remember, your success or failure as a speaker is largely dependent on audience response.

They Should Be Equal in Importance and Parallel in Phrasing

Besides reinforcing and clarifying your central idea, your main points should be equal in importance to each other. Supporting your central idea with two strong points and one weak one will lessen your effectiveness. You will find yourself devoting a considerable amount of time to two points and very little to the third. While you don't have to devote exactly the same amount of time to each point, they should be somewhat near the same length. Also, if you word your main points in a parallel manner, it will emphasize the fact that they are equal in importance. One way to ensure similarity in phrasing is to repeat key words. Compare these two sets of main points for a speech on swimming.

Nonparallel

> *Central idea:* Swimming is beneficial to your health.
> *Main point:* It conditions your mind and your body.
> *Main point:* You exercise most of your muscles.
> *Main point:* The capacity of your lungs is increased.

Parallel

Central idea: Swimming is beneficial to your health.
Main point: It conditions your mind and your body.
Main point: It exercises most of your muscles.
Main point: It increases your lung capacity.

Arranging Central Idea and Main Points

The information that you are presenting to your audience must be organized in such a way that it makes sense to them and can be easily followed. You can organize the central idea and main points that you present in your speech a number of ways. The seven most basic organizational patterns follow:

1. *Chronological order.* Many speeches lend themselves to development in a chronological order. In this pattern you relate a series of incidents or explain a process according to the order in which the incidents or steps in the process occur or have occurred—from first to last. You might analyze the development of rock and roll or demonstrate how to make lasagna.

Example.   *Central idea:* You must follow four steps when making lasagna.

   a. Step 1 involves preparing the meat sauce.
   b. Step 2 includes making and cooking the pasta.
   c. Step 3 involves preparing the three cheeses.
   d. Step 4 is layering the ingredients into baking dishes and baking the lasagna.

2. *General to specific.* In a sense, a general-to-specific pattern is found in most speeches. The central idea, usually given in the introduction, is a general statement, and it is followed by a statement of the main points in less general terms. Finally, each of these main points is supported by specific details. The opposite of this would be a specific-to-general pattern, where the main points are given first and the central idea is stated in the conclusion.

Example A.   *Central idea:* Betty White is an excellent speech teacher.

   a. She has established an excellent rapport with her students and made them enthusiastic about speech.
   b. She has demonstrated her thorough knowledge of the subject along with sound teaching techniques.
   c. She has been able to communicate her understanding of speech to the students and has helped them improve.

Example B

   a. Betty White has established an excellent rapport with her students and made them enthusiastic about speech.
   b. Betty White has demonstrated that she has a thorough knowledge of her subject along with sound teaching techniques.
   c. Betty White has been able to communicate her understanding of speech to the students and has helped them to improve.

   Concluding central idea: Therefore, Betty White is an excellent speech teacher.

3. *Topical.* Sometimes a pattern of arrangement is suggested by the topic itself. For instance, a discussion of music history might logically divide itself into four areas: preclassical, classical, romantic, and contemporary. Similarly, a discussion of a college or university might involve the board of directors, the administration, the faculty, and the student body.

Example.   *Central idea:* The development of music can be roughly divided into four broad areas.

   a. The first is preclassical.
   b. The second is classical.
   c. The third is romantic.
   d. The fourth is contemporary.

4. *Spatial.* A subject might fall quite naturally into a spatial arrangement. An analysis of education in different parts of the country, a demonstration on how to landscape the front of a house, and an explanation of how the body digests foods would lend themselves to this pattern of development.

Example.   *Central idea:* Digestion, the process by which the body absorbs and utilizes food, takes place in three areas of the body.

   a. Digestion begins in the mouth, where the food is ground into a semi-solid mass.
   b. Digestion continues in the stomach, where food becomes a mixed liquid.
   c. Digestion is completed in the small intestines, where the final stage occurs.

5. *Cause and effect.* Although it can be used as an organizational pattern for speeches to entertain or inform, the cause-and-effect pattern is most often used for persuasive speeches. A typical example is that of a salesperson trying to convince a prospective customer that buying the product (cause) will result in all sorts of advantages (effect). Following is an outline of a student speech that utilizes the cause-and-effect pattern to describe the beneficial effects of jogging.

Example.   *Central idea:* Jogging is the ideal exercise.

    a. It conditions the body.
    b. It removes unwanted fat.
    c. It provides emotional balance.

6. *Problem–solution.* Another organizational pattern most often employed in speeches to persuade is the problem-solution order. This speech usually begins with an introduction that states a problem as the central idea of the speech. The body of the speech is organized around the solution or solutions to the problem. Following is a sample outline of a typical problem-solution speech:

Example.   *Central idea:* The amount of money that our student government will receive from outside sources this year has been cut in half, eliminating funding for many of our programs.

    The solution to this problem is to hold a two-day bratwurst festival during the month of October, which will raise enough money to make up the difference.

7. *Motivated sequence.* Monroe's motivated sequence is yet another organizational pattern. It was developed in the 1930s by the late Alan H. Monroe, a speech professor at Purdue University. It lists a five-step plan of action.*

    a. Capture the attention of the audience.
    b. Indicate a need for the audience to listen.
    c. Show how your proposal will satisfy that need.
    d. Visualize what will happen if the plan is put into operation.
    e. Indicate the action you wish your audience to take.

Example.   *Central idea:* Congress must pass a federal law requiring stiffer penalties for drunken driving.

    a. Show pictures of fatal crashes involving drunk drivers.
    b. Cite statistics that emphasize the problem.
    c. Show how tougher laws have worked in other countries.
    d. Describe life without the menace of the drunken driver on the road.
    e. Tell those in your audience to sign your petition.

Speeches that are well organized are clearer and therefore more effective. Using one of the organizational patterns given above will make it easier for

---

*From Douglas Ehninger, Bruce Gronbeck, Ray McKerrow, and Alan Monroe, *Principles and Types of Speech Communication*, 10th ed. (Glenview, IL: Scott Foresman, 1986), p. 153.

those in your audience to understand and remember the information in your speech. You have undoubtedly come in contact with many of these organizational patterns before. That is because the mind is conditioned to organize chronologically, spatially, topically, logically, and from general to specific. Your chances of communicating effectively with your audience will be much greater if you use an organizational pattern that can easily be followed.

Add Appropriate Supporting Material

Supporting materials are necessary for clarifying or proving the points you make in the body of your speech. By themselves the major and subordinate points are really only the structure or skeleton of your speech. It is the quality and relevancy of the supports you choose that make your ideas clear, interesting, and acceptable to your audience. Following is an outline of the body of the speech whose central idea is: Our school cafeteria is an excellent place to eat, to which supporting materials have been added.

Body of Speech

I. The prices are reasonable.
   A. (Testimony) Bernie Koula, the cafeteria manager, has told me how pleased customers are with food prices.
   B. (Statistics/comparison) A student senate survey has determined that area restaurants charge from 20 to 30 percent more for comparable meals.
   C. (Example) I took my friend Chris and his girlfriend, Kathy, to lunch at our cafeteria, and they couldn't believe how low the prices were.
   D. (Visual aid/comparison) Here is an enlargement of a typical breakfast menu from our school cafeteria. When you compare it with these enlarged menus from the two restaurants closest to the school, you can see that the cafeteria's prices are consistently lower.

II. The food is excellent.
   A. It is top quality.
      1. (Testimony) Mrs. Doris Newman, who does the buying for the school cafeteria, has testified that only USDA choice meats and top-quality bakery and produce are purchased by her.
      2. (Explanation) Chef Vivian Sacia, in charge of food preparation for the cafeteria, explains that all food is prepared by second- and third-year students of hotel and restaurant cooking under the watchful eye of their professors.

B. It is well prepared.
   1. (Comparison/testimony) A recent article in the MATC *Times* quoted the governor, who recently toured the college, as saying the meal he ate in the cafeteria was as good as he has had in any school in Wisconsin.
   2. (Example/testimony) I recently took my mother-in-law to the school cafeteria for a birthday lunch. We had tacos and burritos, and my mother-in-law, who is Mexican, said she had never tasted any that were better.

III. The surroundings are neat and clean.

A. The eating area is spotless.
   1. (Explanation) During serving hours cafeteria personnel are ever present, wiping off tables and cleaning up spills. After closing, the entire area is scrubbed thoroughly.
   2. (Example) Last semester I was having lunch in the cafeteria with a group of friends. As one of them was approaching our table, she tripped and dropped her whole tray of food onto the floor. Within minutes the entire mess was cleaned up by two cafeteria workers.

B. The kitchen is immaculate.
   1. (Testimony/comparison) Leif Marking, city health inspector, has stated that in his twenty-six years of inspecting area restaurants he has never found one with a cleaner kitchen.
   2. (Explanation) The kitchen and everything in it is cleaned each evening after closing. Lindsay Degenhardt, a cafeteria worker, has only one assignment, to see that the kitchen stays as clean as possible throughout the day.

Transitions

The body of the speech outlined above consists of main and supporting points, along with supporting material for each. However, in order to move your listeners smoothly from one point to the next, you must include transitions or links between each point. Transitions act like guideposts for your listeners. When you use words like *also* and *in addition* you indicate that your thinking is moving forward. Words like *on the other hand* and *conversely* indicate a reversal of direction. Imagine the following situation: An instructor walks into class and says to her students, "As you all know, you are scheduled to take your midsemester exam in this course today. However . . ." The instructor pauses. An audible sigh of relief is heard throughout the room. The word "however" has caused the students to reverse their thinking. There will be no exam today.

Transitions will help to provide coherence to your speech so that your ideas flow smoothly from one point to the next. Following are a number of suggestions for providing coherence to your speech:

1. Use transitional words: also, again, as a result, besides, but, conversely, however, in addition, in contrast, likewise, moreover, nevertheless, similarly, then, therefore, thus, yet.
2. Use enumerative signposts. "There are three main reasons: first . . . second . . . third. . . ."
   "Point A is this: . . . ."
3. Repeat key words. "Our nuclear buildup isn't defense. Our nuclear buildup is suicide."
4. Conclude your discussion of one point by introducing the next point. "This concludes the discussion of step 2, stripping. Next we will consider step 3, sanding."
5. Begin your discussion of a new point with a reference to the point you just finished discussing. "Now that we have finished our discussion of step 3, sanding, we are ready to move on to step 4, refinishing."

Keep in mind that as a listener you are obliged to do whatever you can to make your ideas as clear and interesting to your listeners as possible. Using effective transitions in your speeches will help you achieve this goal.

Exercises

1. Write out a central idea statement and two or more main points for one or more of the following subjects as your instructor directs.

   a. Restaurants
   b. Hobbies
   c. Sports
   d. Entertainment
   e. Politics
   f. Fitness

Speech Assignment

Relating a Personal Experience to Entertain

Deliver a two- to three-minute speech in which you tell your audience of a personal experience you had that they will find entertaining. Your story can be either entirely true, partly true, or fictitious. It can utilize humor, novelty, the familiar, the startling, the vital, conflict, or suspense to hold the attention of the audience. The important thing is that you describe the situation in enough detail to create a mental picture for your audience.

Delivery

Deliver this speech extemporaneously with no more than one note card. An audience will expect you to have almost total eye contact when talking about your own experiences. The more spontaneous and relaxed you are, the more your audience will enjoy your speech.

Suggested Subjects

1. Camping can be fun, for bears
2. My most embarrassing experience
3. A day I'll never forget
4. I learned to ski the hard way
5. My first date

7

The Introduction and Conclusion

Objectives of Introductions

Now that you have outlined the body of your speech, you are ready to begin developing your introduction. In most cases an introduction to a speech has five objectives: (1) it should capture the audience's attention, (2) it should present the central idea of the speech, (3) it should indicate your qualifications, (4) it should give the audience a reason for listening, and (5) it should preview the ideas to be covered in the speech. Keep in mind that although an introduction will often include all five of these elements, at times one or more of them may be omitted.

1. Capture attention—The first goal of the speaker is to get the attention of the audience. You cannot communicate to an audience that is not paying attention to you. Ten suggestions for getting the attention of your audience are listed as follows. They are designed to put your audience in a good frame of mind and to prepare them to listen to you.

2. Present central idea—You should present the central idea of your speech early in your introduction. It should be a declarative statement about your subject that you must explain or defend rather than a fact that no one can deny. The central idea may be thought of as the key statement or thesis of your speech. It should be worded as a simple sentence. Phrases, questions, or compound and complex sentences are not appropriate for central idea statements.

3. Indicate your qualifications—If you can show your audience that you have appreciable knowledge about your subject, it will motivate them to listen to you. If you've always had an interest in the subject and researched it carefully, reveal this to your audience. If you have had personal experience with a topic, tell them about it. If you are an expert on a subject, don't be modest about it, let them know.

4. Give reason for listening—The next step is to make it clear to the audience why they should listen to your speech. You might show how a problem affects them or others they are concerned about and why they need to listen to your plan for solving the problem; you might explain why the subject is useful to them and how they will gain something by listening; or you might give them some background information that will trigger their curiosity or interest.

5. Preview main points—The preview statement gives your audience a clear explanation of the main ideas to be covered in your speech. It is important because it prepares your audience to listen for and retain key information. The preview statement is the last thing you say in the introduction and should provide a transition into the body of the speech. If you've prepared your speech carefully with your audience in mind, your preview statement will hold the attention of your audience and give them something to look forward to.

Attention Step in Introductions

Besides fulfilling some or all of these objectives, an effective introduction should lead smoothly into the body of the speech. The first objective of the introduction is to get the attention of the audience. Following are ten methods for accomplishing this. Each is followed by a model.

Start off with Humor

When I was preparing this speech, I was reminded of the story of the woman who called up the fire department and screamed, "Come quick! My house is on fire." And when the fireman on the other end of the line responded, "OK lady, but how do we get there?" she replied, "Don't you have that big red truck anymore?" Now that story is kind of silly, but there's also a certain amount of truth to it. It won't be long before fire departments will no longer have red trucks.

Now that science has found that pastel colors are considerably more visible than red, more and more fire departments are changing to yellow or lime-green vehicles. However, this is only one of many changes fire departments have made over the last ten years. Today I'm going to tell you about some of the most interesting of these changes. Some of them, you won't believe.

Begin with a Startling Statement

Even though the dosages would be microscopic, so that you couldn't even see them, if two pounds of plutonium could be evenly distributed among the world's population, each person on earth would receive a lethal dosage. We wouldn't need poison gas or neutron bombs. All we would need is two pounds of plutonium. In spite of this alarming fact, if things continue at the present rate, the United States will be producing seventeen hundred tons of plutonium by the year 2000. Unless we can find more foolproof safeguards for handling the stuff, an enemy won't have to push a button to annihilate us. We will do the job ourselves.

Ask a Rhetorical Question

Do you know what your chances are of getting AIDS? Well, if you are not a member of a high-risk group and do not get involved sexually with a member of a high-risk group, your chances are one in one million. If you are a weekly ticket buyer, those are roughly your chances of being the winner of a state lottery, or put another way, your chances of dying from any other cause are considerably greater. However, AIDS is a disease that has attracted much attention, and there is not a great deal known about it. Today I am going to talk about the symptoms of AIDS, how it is transmitted, and what is being done to combat it.

Begin with a Statistic

Did you know that in this state some districts spend more than $12,000 on their public school students while others in property-poor areas get less than $5,000 a year in support? Poor children in rural Wisconsin and students in Wisconsin's inner city neighborhoods are discriminated against because the property tax rates are higher in these districts than the rates in richer areas. A 1993 Common Cause study blames this inequity on Wisconsin's archaic property tax system which dates back to the days of one-room schools. What can be done about this lack of equal educational opportunities?

Refer to a Previous Speaker

I really enjoyed Nadine's speech on how to save money by buying generic. I had no idea of how many products were sold under the generic label. Some of the comparative prices she quoted were fantastic. What a simple way to save money, too. And who isn't interested in that? In my speech I'm going to show you how you can get the best return on the money you save through buying generic by investing in an IRA. Now you might be saying to yourself,

"I'm too young to be thinking about an IRA." Well, if you listen to me for just a few minutes, I think you will agree that no matter what your age or income, there is an IRA designed just for you.

Start with a Quotation

It was Edmund Burke who said, "The only thing necessary for the triumph of evil is for good men to do nothing." Those words are as true today as they were in the eighteenth century. Many "good" Americans have sat passively by as this nation has continued its status as the world's leading exporter of weapons of destruction, exporting more missiles, aircraft, tanks, and ships than any other country. Rather than seeking peace, the United States has contributed to an arms race unparalleled in the history of the world. The world does not need more weapons of destruction. What is needed is an effective means for resolving conflict. Today I'd like to tell you about some specific things you can do to help stop this arms race.

Begin with a Brief Story

For as long as I can remember, I have loved to fish. We own a summer cottage on a chain of lakes, and because my father is a teacher, we spend the entire summer there. Although I always caught my share of fish, I never did better than my brothers until two years ago. That's when I got the book Lunkers Love Nightcrawlers *for my birthday. Since then, my success with fishing has been phenomenal. It is no longer unusual for me to catch a limit of bass or walleyes after a full day of fishing. But the secret isn't in living on a lake and knowing where to fish. The secret lies in knowing how to fish with nightcrawlers effectively. This morning I'm going to pass on to you a few of the secrets I've learned from* Lunkers Love Nightcrawlers, *an amazing book.*

Refer to the Familiar

I'll bet there isn't a person in this room who hasn't been called an insulting name at one time or other. Some of the kids on our block used to call me fatty when I was younger because I was a chubby little guy. Well that really hurt, and I'll bet when you were called a name it hurt you too. Can you imagine how it hurts Native Americans to be called Redskins, Redmen, and Braves? People need to stand up and take this issue seriously. Here's what you can do to help.

List a Series of Examples

On their way home from a family reunion a young couple and their infant son are killed in a head-on collision with a pickup truck that crosses the cen-

ter line. Two weeks later, an eight-year-old girl is crippled for life by a car that jumps the curb, crashes through a fence, and veers into the yard where she is playing. The next day, after leaving a party, a teenage girl and her drunken boyfriend are thrown from his motorcycle and killed when he fails to negotiate a dangerous curve. What do these accidents have in common? They were all caused by drivers who were intoxicated. They are typical stories that appear in newspapers day after day in cities throughout our nation. And the greatest tragedy is that many of these kinds of accidents would never happen again if we could do one thing: find a way to get the drunk driver off the road.

Begin with a Definition

Many people think of child abuse as an injury to a child resulting from a physical or sexual act. However, this is only one form of abuse. Dr. C. Henry Kempe of the University of Colorado Medical Center, a recognized authority on child abuse, has defined a victim as "any child who receives nonaccidental injury or injuries as a result of acts or omissions on the part of his parents or guardians." That means that if a child is injured as a result of not being fed properly or because of being left unattended, the person responsible is as guilty as one who has inflicted physical violence on a child. Making people more aware of exactly what constitutes child abuse would help in dealing with the problem. It's time we brought child abuse out of the closet and into the spotlight where it belongs.

The list of suggestions given above for attention-getting introductions is by no means complete. Other methods include referring to a recent event or one that is soon to take place, a buildup of suspense, the use of a visual aid as part of the introduction, the use of novelty or the unusual, an introduction involving conflict, and establishing a common ground with the audience.

Choose your introduction carefully. It should be consistent with the purpose and the central idea of your speech. A humorous introduction to a serious speech would be a poor choice. Be aware that the introduction is the first thing your audience hears, and therefore it has much to do with the effectiveness of your speech.

Types of Conclusions

Some people feel that the conclusion is the most important part of the speech. It is your last chance to achieve your purpose, and it signals to your audience that your speech is ending. Plan your conclusion carefully. It is the final impression the audience will get of your speech, and it should leave them with a sense of completeness. It is no accident that many of the most memorable lines from speeches have occurred at or near the conclusion. Among them are the following:

> *I know not what course others may take, but as for me, give me liberty, or give me death!*
>
> —*Patrick Henry*

> *That we here highly resolve that these dead shall not have died in vain—that this nation, under God, shall have a new birth of freedom—and that the government of the people, by the people, and for the people shall not perish from the earth.*
>
> —*Abraham Lincoln*

> *Ask not what your country can do for you; ask what you can do for your country.*
>
> —*John F. Kennedy*

Finally, remember never to introduce new material in your conclusion. To do so will leave your audience with the impression that you failed to plan your speech carefully and added the new material as an afterthought, or that you left something out of your talk and remembered it just as you were about to close. Either way, you wind up with egg on your face. Following are six suggestions for effectively concluding your speech:

End with a Restatement of Your Central Idea

A speech that has as its central idea, We must bring child abuse out of the closet and into the spotlight, might end this way:

> *Because there has been a steady increase in child abuse in the United States during the 1990s, because in some of our states the penalties are stiffer for abusing animals than for abusing children, and because many people are not aware of what does or does not constitute child abuse, there must be an immediate and concerted effort made to address this problem—through litigation, through communication, through education, and through cooperation. We must pull child abuse out of the darkness and put it into the spotlight so that we can see it for the evil that it is.*

End with a Summary of the Main Ideas Developed in Your Speech

A speech with the central idea, Our school cafeteria is an excellent place to eat, might conclude this way:

I imagine that by now you've come to the conclusion that I'm sold on our cafeteria, and you're right. But I have good reasons. When I went to grade school and high school I took a bag lunch most of the time. Not that the food wasn't good at those schools; it was. My mom just did a super job with the sandwiches and all the rest. Then I got to our school, tried the cafeteria, and that was it. That's where I eat while I'm at school because the prices are reasonable, the food is excellent, and the surroundings are neat and clean.

End with a Call to Action

The speech that has as its central idea, We must get the drunk driver off the road, might end this way:

As I said earlier, I am not taking a pie-in-the-sky approach to this problem. Drunk drivers have been on the road since the horse-and-buggy days, and there will probably be someone operating flying saucers while under the influence. However, in spite of the fact that our legislators are dragging their feet in passing tougher laws, in spite of the fact that there are too many loopholes in present laws, and in spite of the fact that in many cases law enforcement is neither uniform nor strict enough, MADD, Mothers Against Drunk Driving, has made a difference. Slowly but surely, laws are getting tougher, the loopholes are being plugged, and enforcement is getting stricter and more uniform. By supporting MADD, you will be helping to get the drunk driver off the road. For as little as five dollars per year you can become a sustaining member. Pick up a membership blank from me at the end of our meeting today. Then, send it in along with your check or money order. The life you save may be your own or that of a loved one.

End with a Rhetorical Question

A speech with the central idea, We need foolproof safeguards for stockpiling and handling plutonium, might end this way:

Can the United States afford to manufacture and store a substance so deadly that a few ounces of it could destroy every living creature on this continent? The answer is obvious. However, our government has not yet responded. Haven't we learned anything from the space shuttle tragedy? How many more will have to die before we set up fail-safe systems? Write your representatives in the House and Senate now and tell them that we need foolproof safeguards for stockpiling and handling plutonium.

End with a Positive Vision of the Future

The vision of the future that you project can be either positive or negative. The choice is up to you. For instance, in a problem–solution speech, you can visualize for your audience what the future will be like once the problem is solved. The following excerpt is the positive view of the future envisioned by Dr. Martin Luther King, Jr., in his stirring speech "I Have a Dream."

> *From every mountainside let freedom ring. And when this happens, and when we allow freedom to ring, when we let it ring from every village and every hamlet, from every state and every city, we will be able to speed up that day when all of God's children, black men and white men, Jews and gentiles, Protestants and Catholics, will be able to join hands and sing in the words of the old Negro spiritual, free at last. Free at last. Thank God almighty, we are free at last!*

End with a Negative Vision of the Future

There may be times when you will want to leave your audience with the feeling that the problem must be solved before it is too late. In these cases you might want to paint a picture of what the future will be like if something is not done to solve the problem as soon as possible. A speech with the central idea, Can the lower-income American family survive? might end with this negative vision of the future:

> *Unless we reverse the rising tide of poverty in this country, millions of families will disintegrate, not just break up. Child abuse and violence in the home will become epidemic as parents turn to alcohol and drugs to escape their problems and then return home to physically release their anger on their children or each other. Others who can't make it will place their children in foster homes or institutions or just simply abandon them. The potential for having the whole support system for families collapse is very real. We're seeing it now, and unless we do something about it very soon, the answer to the question I asked at the beginning of this speech, Can the lower-income American family survive? will be a tragic but resounding no!*

Other suggestions for concluding your speech are to end with a quotation, a poem, a story, a startling statement, a visual aid, a combination of methods, or an epigram.

Outlining Your Speech

Although outlining your speech involves extra work, the rewards are worth it. The major benefit of an outline is that it allows you to check your speech for potential mistakes. A speech outline is essentially a plan of what you want to say. Carefully examining your outline will help ensure that the main points of your speech clarify or reinforce your central idea, cover your subject adequately, are equal in importance, and are worded in a similar way. In addition, an outline will enable you to assess whether your subpoints and supporting materials are adequate and sufficiently varied and whether your introduction and conclusion are appropriate to the body of your speech. Finally, an outline will help you determine where transitions might be needed. There are two types of outlines that may be helpful for developing and delivering your speech: (1) a planning outline, and (2) a delivery outline. This section will deal with the planning outline from which a delivery outline can be developed.

Planning Outline

Keep in mind, what you put down in a planning outline is only tentative. It can always be changed. You can't expect to come up with a finished product on your first try. You will probably wind up with a number of rough drafts before you decide on one you like. When your outline is complete, you will have the skeleton for your speech. The following guidelines will be helpful when developing a planning outline.

- Divide outline into three parts.
- Use standard outline form.
- Write out your main points.
- Support each main point.
- Develop your conclusion.
- Develop your introduction.
- Add transitions.

Divide Outline into Three Parts: Introduction, Body and Conclusion

A speech should be divided into three parts: the introduction, the body, and the conclusion. Each of these three parts has a specific function. The introduction should get your audience's attention, give them a reason for listening, indicate your central idea and qualifications, and preview your subject. The body should communicate your ideas clearly and meaningfully, and the conclusion should restate your central ideas and main points and tie them together in a neat package. "In other words," as a wag once said, "in your intro, you tell the people what you're going to tell 'em; in the body, you tell 'em what you said you'd tell 'em, and in the conclusion, you tell 'em what you've told 'em."

Use Standard Outline Form

Standard outline form requires that you write your outline in complete sentences and follow the rules of coordination and subordination. Coordination means that all statements at the same level in your outline are equal in importance. Subordination means that each statement in your outline supports the statement in the level directly above it.

Outline numbering follows this order:

I. Main Point Number 1 (Roman numerals)

  A. Supporting Point (Capital letters)
    1. Supporting Material (Arabic numerals)
      a. Evidence (Small letters)
      b. Evidence

  B. Supporting Point
    2. Supporting Material
      a. Evidence
      b. Evidence

II. Main Point Number 2

Indent all headings in the outline. Place numbers and letters of all headings directly under the first word of the heading above. Roman numerals for main points are placed closest to the left margin. Note that the periods following the Roman numerals line up directly below each other. Putting your ideas into this outline form allows you to see the relationship between main points, supporting points, subpoints, and supporting materials in your speech. Thus, you can judge whether main points are worded similarly and are approximately equal in importance; whether all points at a given level have about the same amount of support; and whether each level in the outline is related to the level above it.

Write Out Your Main Points

The main points should be written as complete sentences and should clarify or reinforce your central idea. Combined, they should cover your subject adequately. They should be equal in importance and worded in a similar way. Your main points should be numbered in standard outline form. A speech with the central idea, Rocks make great pets, might be supported with these four main points:

I. They are inexpensive.
II. They are easy to care for.
III. They are fun to watch.
IV. They're great to throw when you want to let off steam.

Support Each Main Point

Each main point in your speech requires specific supporting material. Supporting materials are necessary to make your ideas clear or convincing to your audience. As a rule of thumb, the more controversial your main point is, the more supporting material you will need to back it up. In any event, each main point should be supported by at least two supporting points. If you can't find at least two supports for a main point, it probably should be omitted. Supporting points should be supported by subpoints and so on.

Keep in mind that some speeches may have only one main point. A short speech to persuade with the central idea, Never buy anything sight unseen, might involve you telling your audience about an experience you had that taught a lesson that was the single main point of your speech: "I learned at an early age never to buy anything I hadn't seen first." You might deliver a speech of personal experience to entertain with a central idea that is also the main point: "Camping can be fun, for bears!"

Develop Your Conclusion

A conclusion should be short and to the point. It should comprise from 5 to 10 percent of the total speech and include one or any combination of the following: a summary of the main points, a restatement of the central idea, a question, a call to action, a vision of the future, and so on.

Develop Your Introduction

The minimum purpose of any introduction should be to get the audience's attention and reveal your subject. However, most introductions should have five objectives: (1) to capture the audience's attention, (2) to present the central idea of the speech, (3) to indicate your qualifications for giving the speech, (4) to give the audience a reason for listening, and (5) to preview the ideas to be covered in the speech. As a rule of thumb, the introduction should comprise only 10 to 15 percent of the total speech time.

Add Transitions

An effective speech must be coherent; that is, the ideas must relate to each other as parts of the whole. A coherent speech is one with transitions or links between main and supporting ideas. Suggestions for providing coherence to your speech with transitions are found on pages 66–121.

Sample Full-Sentence Outline for a Speech to Actuate

Sample Outline

Following is a model complete-sentence outline on the benefits of walking:

> Purpose: To persuade my listeners that walking is the perfect exercise.
> Organizational pattern: Cause and effect

Introduction

I. (Testimony) Over 2000 years ago Hippocates, the father of medicine said, "Walking is man's best medicine." (Attention-getting quotation)

II. (Explanation) Many feel that with heart disease the number one killer in the country and with over one-fourth of the population significantly overweight, exercise is the only hope. (Reason for listening)

III. (Testimony) The National Institute of Health says, "Walking is the ideal exercise (central idea) and the only one you can safely follow all the years of your life."

IV. (Explanation) After many hours of research, I have found that anyone can walk, the young and old, sick and healthy, male and female. (Indicating qualifications)

V. (Preview statement) Today I'm going to show you that walking is the ideal exercise because it strengthens the heart and conditions a person both mentally and physically.

(Transition: The first, and perhaps most important thing, that walking does is to strengthen the heart.)

Body

I. Walking strengthens the heart.

  A. It improves collateral circulation.

  1. (Explanation-visual aid) When some arteries become narrowed by fatty deposits, those nearby get wider and open up new branches to maintain an adequate blood supply.

  2. (Testimony) Dr. Samuel Fox, president of the American College of Cardiology says walking increases the number and size of your blood vessels and the efficiency of the heart.

  3. (Example) Steve McKanic was told at the age of forty-six that his heart condition was incurable and there was no hope. He started walking, and five years later he's active and healthy again.

  4. (Statistic) It is estimated that twelve million people in this country are being treated for heart disease and twelve million more have it and don't know it.

  B. It lowers blood pressure.

  1. (Explanation-visual aid) Muscles in your feet, calves, thighs, buttocks, and abdomen help push seventy-two thousand quarts of

blood through your system every twenty-four hours. These muscles are exercised by walking, making them more efficient and thus lowering your blood pressure.

2. (Example) Natalie Smith had such high blood pressure her doctor was afraid to let her drive a car because he thought she would have a stroke. She started walking, and a year later her blood pressure was normal.

3. (Testimony) A recent study by Dr. Kenneth Cooper, author of *Aerobics*, demonstrates the connection between a person's fitness level and high blood pressure.

4. (Example) Eula Weaver suffered her first high-blood-pressure-related heart attack at age seventy-eight. Today at eighty-nine she walks regularly, and her blood pressure is normal.

(Transition: Second, walking helps to condition a person mentally by reducing stress and improving self-image.)

II. Walking conditions a person mentally.
   A. It reduces stress.
      1. (Testimony-comparison) Dr. Herbert DeVries, University of California physiologist, concluded after a university study that a fifteen-minute walk reduced neuromuscular tension more effectively than a standard dose of tranquilizers.
      2. (Example) Albert Einstein, Harry Truman, and Abraham Lincoln walked daily to escape from the tension of their jobs.
      3. (Testimony) Dr. Paul Dudley White, dean of American cardiologists, said, "A minimum of an hour a day of fast walking is absolutely necessary for one's optimal health, including that of the brain."
      4. (Testimony-comparison) Dr. Hans Selye's well-known experiment on the effects of psychological stress on sedentary and active rats demonstrates the effectiveness of physical conditioning in combating stress.
   B. It improves self-image.
      1. (Testimony) After a company-sponsored program of walking for twenty minutes twice daily, the thirty women involved said they felt better, happier, and more productive.
      2. (Testimony) "Walking," says psychologist John Martin, "helps you function more efficiently because you know you are doing

something positive and constructive, and this makes you feel better about yourself."

3. (Example) Aunt Rose, who has tried unsuccessfully to lose weight for years, started walking and in nine months went from a size 22 to size 14. She is a new person.

4. (Explanation) Walking improves circulation, sending more oxygen to the brain and creating a euphoria that improves self-concept. (Transition: Finally, walking conditions a person physically by aiding in weight control and improving physical fitness.)

III. Walking conditions a person physically.

   A. It removes unwanted fat.

      1. (Visual aid) This chart indicates the number of calories a person of a particular weight will expend in an hour by walking between two and five miles per hour.

      2. (Statistical testimony) Dr. Charles T. Kuntzleman, national fitness consultant to the YMCA, estimates that there are presently fifty million Americans who are seriously obese.

      3. (Example) Three-hundred-pound Molly Ryan, who claimed to have a glandular problem that kept her fat, began walking after a heart attack and lost one hundred pounds after the first year.

      4. (Comparison) Time-and-motion studies indicate that the typical overweight person walks 2.8 miles per day, compared to 4.8 miles per day for a person of normal weight.

   B. It improves a person's fitness.

      1. (Testimony) Dr. Lawrence Golding conducted a controlled experiment with twenty-five women at Kent State University in which he found that walking combined with dieting was far superior to dieting alone in its effect on physical fitness.

      2. (Comparison) A study of the health records of thirty-one thousand double-decker-bus workers in London found that the fare collectors, who walked around the bus and climbed the stairs regularly, had a much lower mortality rate and faster recovery from heart attacks than the inactive bus drivers.

      3. (Example) Scrambling over the slopes of their mountainous homeland has given the long-lived citizens of Hunza in the Himalayas such a high degree of cardiovascular fitness that even when they get a heart attack, it does little harm.

4. (Visual aid) This chart, devised by the Michigan Heart Association, will help you determine whether or not lack of fitness is increasing your chances of having a heart attack.
   (Transition: You have heard about the benefits of walking for the young or old, male or female, and sick or healthy. All you really need for this exercise program are your two feet.)

Conclusion

I. (Explanation) It is obvious that exercise is necessary to add years to your life and life to your years.
II. (Comparison) It doesn't matter which exercise you use as long as it moves you into the good or excellent fitness category.
III. (Explanation) Walking is the easiest and most efficient way for anyone to get fit and stay fit and everyone can use it.
IV. (Explanation) Walking is an exercise that will strengthen your heart and improve both your mental and physical fitness.

Bibliography

Books:
Allsen, P. E. and Harrison, J. M. *Fitness For Life*. Dubuque, Iowa: William C. Brown, 1976.
Kuntzleman, Charles T. *The Complete Book of Walking*. New York: Simon & Schuster, 1978.
Man, John. *Walk!* New York: Paddington Press Ltd., 1979.

Periodicals:
Conniff, J. C. "Getting on a Good Footing." *New York Times Magazine*, April 23, 1978.
Goldstein, J. "Walkers of the World, Unite!" *Fitness for Living*, May/June 1986.
Howorth, D. "The Art of Walking." *Consumer Bulletin*, April 1978.
McDermott, B. "Going Through Life at a Walk." *Sports Illustrated*, May 8, 1978.

Although an outline for your speech similar to the one above involves a great deal of preparation, it is important for a number of reasons. First, it provides a logical arrangement of your main points and subpoints along with an idea of the supporting materials you are going to use. This will enable you to determine whether your ideas flow smoothly from one to another, and whether you have included a well-balanced and sufficient number of the six kinds of supporting materials. Second, it will provide a framework from which you can prepare note cards or a phrase outline, or from which you can write out a speech to be delivered from manuscript or from memory.

This outline includes a bibliography. While many of the speeches you deliver will involve your own experience, there are times when you will want to include materials you have gathered through research. In these cases, or whenever your instructor so directs, attach a bibliography to your preparation outline.

Exercises

1. Develop alternative introductions for an upcoming speech using the suggestions given in this chapter for getting and holding the attention of your audience.
2. Develop alternative conclusions for an upcoming speech using the suggestions given in this chapter for successfully concluding your speech.
3. Write out a complete sentence outline for an upcoming speech.

Speech Assignment

Relating a Personal Experience to Make a Point
Develop a three- to four-minute speech in which you describe an experience you had that taught you a lesson. The story may be true, partly true, or fictitious. Develop your material informally with emphasis on details of action.

Delivery
This speech should be delivered extemporaneously. Use no more than one note card. An audience will expect you to have almost total eye contact when telling of your own experiences.

Sample Central Ideas

1. Taking a chance can pay off.
2. A first aid course can save someone.
3. Seatbelts save lives.
4. Don't judge a person on the basis of your first meeting.

8

Preparing for Delivery

After you have finished organizing the content of your speech, you are ready to prepare it for delivery. The manner in which you prepare your speech will depend on the method of delivery you choose. Impromptu speeches (those delivered on the spur of the moment) are either not prepared at all or prepared very hastily. Manuscript speeches are written out completely. Memorized speeches are usually written first and then committed to memory. The extemporaneous speech is carefully prepared but delivered without having been written out or memorized. In most situations it is by far the best method of delivery. Besides providing spontaneity, it will enable you to adapt the message to your audience as you are speaking to them and to modify it in response to their feedback.

When you deliver a speech in class, you are communicating in a friendly atmosphere. You are speaking to fellow students who can empathize with you because they are in the same situation as you are. Under these circumstances a speaker should feel relaxed and at ease—but many don't. Why? Many beginning speakers see the situation as threatening rather than friendly. They worry that their classmates will see their shortcomings and imperfections, real or imaginary. Worrying too much about what other people will think of you can cause nervousness.

This is not to say, however, that you should not be concerned with what your listeners will think of your speech. You have good reason to be nervous if you deliver a speech for which you have done little to prepare or practice. While most listeners will expect you to make mistakes while delivering your speech, especially if you are a beginning speaker, few will react favorably to your presentation if they feel it has involved little effort on your part. It is not hard to understand why those who are poorly prepared suffer from nervousness.

You have a number of options available when you choose to speak extemporaneously. The two most common of these are: (1) develop a delivery outline of key words and phrases from your complete sentence outline and deliver the speech from it, or (2) formulate note cards containing key words from your complete sentence outline and deliver the speech from them. Following is a sample delivery outline made from the complete sentence outline on pages 79–83. At first glance it may appear to have little meaning. Keep in mind, however, that it is meaningful to the speaker and provides signals as to the structure, the ideas, and the direction of the speech.

Sample Delivery Outline

   I. Over 2000, Hippocrates
  II. Heart disease #1
 III. NIH—most efficient
 IV. Everyone can
     A. E. Orstatt
     B. Neighbors
   V. (Central idea) Strengthens heart, conditions mentally, physically (The first . . . strengthens)

Body

   I. Strengthens heart
     A. Collateral circulation
        1. Wider—new branches
        2. Dr. Fox—number, size
        3. Steve McKanic
        4. 12 million know/don't
     B. Blood pressure
        1. Visual aid
        2. Nathalie Smith
        3. Cooper—fitness—HBP
        4. Eula Weaver
(Secondly . . . stress, self-image)
  II. Conditions mentally
     A. Reduces stress
        1. Dr. deVries—neuromuscular tension
        2. Einstein, Truman, Lincoln

   3. Dr. White—1 hour—brain
   4. Dr. Selyes—rats
   B. Improves image
   1. 30 women
   2. Dr. Martin (read quote)
   3. Aunt Rose (22–14)
   4. Oxygen—euphoria
(Finally . . . physically)
III. Conditions physically
   A. Unwanted fat
   1. Visual aid
   2. Dr. Kuntzleman—50 million
   3. Molly Ryan (100 lbs)
   4. TM studies (2.8–4.8)
   B. Fitness
   1. Dr. Golding (25 women)
   2. 31,000 bus workers
   3. Hunza in Himalayas
   4. Visual aid
(You have heard . . .)

Conclusion

   I. Years to life/life to years
  II. Doesn't matter which
 III. Easiest, most efficient, everyone
  IV. Strengthens mentally, physically

Using Note Cards

Many extemporaneous speakers choose to deliver their speeches from note cards rather than from a delivery outline, because they offer several advantages. Note cards are easier to handle than a sheet of paper and are less noticeable. They won't waver if your hand trembles slightly. Note cards are especially helpful if you must deliver your speech without a lectern, because you can hold the cards in one hand and still be able to gesture freely. Here are a number of suggestions to follow when using note cards:

1. Use standard three-by-five-, four-by-six-, or five-by-eight-inch note cards. The number of cards you use will depend on the length and complexity of your speech. If you choose to make your own cards rather than buy them, use rigid paper or cardboard.

2. Always use note cards as unobtrusively as possible except when reading a direct quotation or complicated statistics. In these cases hold your notes up so that your audience can see you are taking special care to be accurate.

3. Make sure your notes are legible. Note cards are easy to read when they are typed or printed in capital letters and double or triple spaced.

4. Number multiple note cards. That way you will be able to put them in order quickly if you happen to drop them or find they are disarranged.

5. Write on only one side of your note card. Even though your audience will expect you to use notes when delivering your speech, turning the cards over is distracting and time consuming.

6. Avoid writing your notes in too much detail. Note cards should serve only as a guide when delivering your speech. The extemporaneous method requires good eye contact and spontaneity. Overly detailed notes might tempt you to read your speech.

7. Avoid putting too much down on each card. Except for cards on which you have written full quotations or a set of statistics, limit to five the number of lines you put on a card. That way you'll be able to find your place in an instant. Remember, except for direct quotations and complicated statistics, the notes are there to jog your memory. Longer speeches will just require more cards.

8. Highlight ideas you wish to stress. Circle or underline key words so that you will remember to emphasize them while delivering your speech. It is often helpful to make notations on your note cards to "pause" or "slow down" at different times during your speech.

Figure 8-1 is a sample note card that could be used to substitute for a section of the delivery outline above. It begins with the transition from the introduction to the body of the speech. Note that although the wording is similar to the keyword outline, the symbols of outlining, Roman numerals, capital letters and so on are left out.

Extemporaneous Method

By far the most effective method of delivering a speech is the extemporaneous method. You know what it is you are going to say, but you haven't written it out or memorized it word for word. In order to be effective in delivering an extemporaneous speech, you must use language that is clear, interesting, and appropriate.

Clarity

While clarity is important in all communication, it is indispensable to speech. A reader can reread a passage as many times as necessary to understand it.

---

(3)

(THE FIRST . . . STRENGTHENS)

COLLATERAL CIRCULATION—WIDER—NEW BRANCHES

Dr. FOX (NUMBER—SIZE) STEVEN McKANIK

12 MILLION   KNOW/DON'T   VISUAL AID

FIGURE 8-1   Sample Note Card

For the listener it must be instantly understood or it is gone. If too much of what you say is missed or misinterpreted, your communication will fail. You can achieve clarity in speaking by (1) using an oral style, (2) choosing concrete rather than abstract words, and (3) using specific rather than general words.

Oral Style

Beginning speakers often phrase main ideas and subpoints in a stilted, unnatural way, usually because they have composed their ideas in a written rather than an oral style. While similarities exist between the two styles, there are also significant differences. For this reason, whenever you write a central idea, scope statement, main point or subpoint, and so on, always read it aloud to make sure it sounds like you are talking in a conversational way. Following are some of the most common characteristics of an oral style:

1. An oral style is replete with contractions. Although in writing, *will not* and *it is* are often preferred to the contractions *won't* and *it's*, contractions are common to an oral style.
2. Oral sentences are usually shorter and less complex than written sentences. Your English teachers insisted that you use longer and more complex sentences in your writing to achieve variety. However, variety can be achieved nonverbally in speech, and overly long sentences cause problems for both speakers and listeners.
3. Oral sentences usually employ a subject–verb order. A common method for achieving variety in writing is to combine normal, periodic, parallel, and balanced sentences. In speaking, the normal sentence (subject–verb pattern) occurs far more frequently than any other type.
4. An oral style uses many familiar words. Always remember that when you are communicating your ideas, you must choose words that mean

the same things to your listeners as they do to you. In most cases the best language to use in speaking is the simplest and most familiar.

5. An oral style makes frequent use of personal pronouns. The use of *us, we, our, you,* and *I* is typical of what is called a conversational speech style. They give the speech an air of familiarity, as if the speaker is talking "with" the audience rather than "to" it.

Concrete Words

Concrete words refer to specific objects or particular instances, things that are relatively easy to visualize or define. They differ from abstract words, which refer to concepts, ideas, or emotions and often mean different things to different people. *Dog, book, rose, World War II,* and *Easter* are concrete words. *Democracy, communism, love,* and *hate* are abstract words. Obviously, a concrete word will always be clearer to your audience than an abstract one. Whenever possible, choose concrete rather than abstract words for your speech. When you must use abstract terms, define them as clearly and as completely as you can.

Specific Words

Another way to achieve clarity in your speaking is to choose specific rather than general words. General words refer to a group or class of things. Specific words refer to a particular part of that group. Specific words are always clearer. Imagine going to your favorite butcher shop and asking for two pounds of meat. How can the butcher fill your order without knowing what kind of meat you want? Two pounds of beef is better but still not specific enough. Do you want hamburger, ground chuck, rib roast, pot roast, or eye of round? Even if you say steak, you leave the butcher wondering which one of a dozen or more kinds of steak you mean. When wording your speech, do your audience and yourself a favor and be as specific as you can.

Interest

An effective way to make your speeches more interesting is to use words that appeal to any of the five senses: sight, hearing, taste, touch, and smell. For example, while it might be perfectly accurate to tell your listeners that a man came toward you, it would be much more visual and therefore more interesting to them if you told them that he staggered, lurched, inched, or crawled. In the same manner, the "eager buzz" of excited fans at a homecoming game and the spicy red chili that heats the mouth and causes perspiration to rise from the pores of the brow present vivid images to those listeners who can relate to them through one or more of their senses.

A second way of adding interest to your speeches is to use descriptive language to present a clear and definite word picture of what is taking place.

Note the following two statements: (1) I sat next to a pretty blonde. (2) I sat next to a tall, slender, tanned blonde with a round and radiant face and dark, inviting eyes. Which statement is more likely to hold attention and establish a clear mental picture?

A third way to make your speeches interesting is to use an attention-getting technique called the *real*—talking in terms of actual people and places. This technique involves giving names to the characters you describe in your stories. For example, it is easier to imagine yourself sitting next to "Sheldon" or "Juanita" than next to your "friend." One can more easily picture your being attacked by the neighbor's vicious boxer, Cruncher, than by the "dog next door."

Finally, you can make your speeches interesting by using the active rather than the passive voice. An added benefit is that besides being more vigorous, the active voice is usually less wordy. Note the following examples:

Passive: *First, the water was boiled by Jane, and then the eggs were added. (13 words)*

Active: *Jane boiled the water first and then added the eggs. (10 words)*

Passive: *The rapist was shot by the intended victim. (8 words)*

Active: *The intended victim shot the rapist. (6 words)*

Appropriateness

When presenting your speech, you must always use language appropriate to your audience and the occasion. It would obviously be inappropriate to use sophisticated scientific terminology in explaining the problems faced in rocket liftoff to a group of laypeople. Not so obvious would be the use of electrical terms (even though simple) in a demonstration speech to a general audience on how to install a 220 outlet.

Unless you know your audience extremely well and the occasion warrants it, it is best to avoid off-color stories or profanity. Always keep in mind that you are speaking to a captive audience. While you might capture the attention of some in your audience with the startling use of a four-letter word or ribald story, any advantage you gain will be negated if you make others uncomfortable or antagonized.

Finally, except in cases where you make it obvious that you are deviating for a special effect, always observe the rules of correct grammar. An audience will forgive or even miss an occasional slip, but if your speech contains too many errors it will affect your credibility. Like it or not, one variable by which an audience tends to judge the competence of speakers is by their correct or incorrect use of language.

Practicing the Speech

Regardless of whether you deliver your speech extemporaneously, from manuscript, or from memory, the key to doing so effectively is practice. Here are some suggestions for practicing your speeches:

1. Allow ample time for practice. Practice delivering your speech from two to five times. The idea is to practice enough to develop an easy and natural delivery but not to the extent that you unintentionally memorize an extemporaneous or manuscript speech.

2. Always practice with the same key-word outline, note cards, or manuscript that you plan to use when delivering your speech. If you retype something, run it through a practice session to make sure you haven't typed in an error or left something out.

3. Always practice your speech as if you were delivering it to your intended audience. After you have practiced alone a few times, try to find a person or two to serve as your audience.

4. Go through the entire speech during each practice. If you hit a trouble spot or two during practice, don't stop and start over. Chances are that if you do, you might do this while delivering your speech. Like it or not, the actual delivery of the speech is more stressful than practice. Don't give yourself any unnecessary handicaps.

5. Do not try to deliver your speech the same way each time you practice it. Whether your speech is extemporaneous, manuscript, or memorized, an important characteristic is spontaneity. Delivering an extemporaneous speech the same way each time might cause you to unintentionally memorize the words. Delivering a manuscript or memorized speech the same way each time could inhibit your vocal variety.

6. Do not coordinate specific gestures with the exact wording of your speech. To be effective, gestures must be spontaneous. While you should practice your speech with the kinds of emphatic and descriptive gestures you will be using in its delivery, don't pinpoint the exact moment to raise your index finger or dust off your shoulder during a speech. A planned or stilted gesture is worse than no gesture at all.

7. Practice your speech aloud with the same volume you plan to use in delivering it. Don't go over the speech in your head or say it so softly that no one can hear you.

8. However, some find it helpful to practice their speech mentally as well as aloud. If this method works for you, use it.

9. Practice your speech each time with whatever visual aids you plan to use. If you plan to mix some ingredients together during your speech, mix them during at least one practice session. This will help prevent slipups.

10. Time your speech in practice. No one appreciates a speech that goes on and on interminably. If you have been given a specific time limit for your speech, conform to it while practicing. As a safeguard, arrange for a friend in the audience to signal you when you have only one minute or so left.

11. Practice the way you will approach the speaker's stand at the beginning of the speech and leave it at the conclusion.

12. If you have access to a tape or video recorder, use it. Recorders are excellent aids. The best audience you can have is you, provided you have learned to listen to yourself critically and objectively.

13. If possible, try to practice at least once in the room where you will be delivering your speech or a similar room. Anything you can do in practice to approximate the real thing is worth the effort.

Exercises

Speech Assignments

1. *Reading a commercial.* Read a one-minute radio or TV commercial that you have written yourself or picked up from a local broadcaster. Study it carefully to decide how to best indicate meaning. Practice it so that you can deliver it easily and naturally.

Delivery. The job of the reader is to communicate sincerity and enthusiasm in an interesting way. You can do this best by using conversational style. Be yourself.

2. *Reading poetry.* Select poetry that falls within a one-to-two-minute time limit. Pick something you think your listeners will like and that you can handle intelligently. Study it carefully in regard to mood and purpose. Practice it so that you can read it effectively.

Delivery. Speak clearly and distinctly using variations in pitch, volume, rate, and inflection to make your reading interesting. Know your selection well enough so that you can maintain adequate eye contact.

3. *Reading prose.* Select a piece of prose that falls within a one-to-two-minute time limit. Pick something you think your listeners will like and that you can handle intelligently. Study it carefully in regard to mood and purpose. Practice it so that you can read it effectively.

Delivery. Speak clearly and distinctly using variations in pitch, volume, rate, and inflection to make your reading interesting. Know your selection well enough so that you can maintain adequate eye contact.

9

Delivery

Once you have determined your purpose and subject, analyzed your audience, developed the content of your speech, prepared it for delivery, and practiced it, you are finished with the hardest part of your job. However, all the work you have done will be wasted if you fail to deliver your speech effectively.

Your method of delivery may vary, depending on a number of variables such as the purpose of your speech, the subject, the occasion, and your audience. Most of the time you will want to deliver your speeches extemporaneously. This is usually the best and most effective method. However, in some instances you might be required to deal with so many facts and statistics that you will want to write your speech out completely and deliver it verbatim so as not to run the risk of forgetting anything. On the other hand, you might be one of those gifted few who have the kind of retention and acting ability needed for delivering an effective memorized speech. If you are lucky, you will not be required at some future date to deliver an impromptu speech with no preparation at all. In case that happens, however, a number of suggestions are offered in this chapter to help you manage more effectively in that difficult situation.

As I have indicated, there are four principal methods of delivery: (1) impromptu, (2) manuscript, (3) memorized, and (4) extemporaneous.

Impromptu Speeches

An impromptu speech is one that is developed on the spur of the moment. It demands a great deal of the speaker since it seldom gives time for advanced thought or preparation. When delivering an impromptu speech, you have little time, if any, to analyze the subject, audience, or occasion. You must think on your feet to choose and organize your material. While this can impart spontaneity and directness to your delivery, it can also result in inappropriate statements, unexpressed thoughts, and repetitiveness. Consider your own experience. How many times have you looked back at a situation and thought, "Why didn't I say that?" or realized that you had put your foot in your mouth and said the wrong thing?

There are times, however, when it is necessary to deliver an impromptu speech. If that situation arises, consider the following advice: (1) keep your speech short and to the point; (2) try to use illustrations for supporting material (from personal experience if possible); (3) handle only one main point; and (4) make sure your central idea and purpose are absolutely clear to your audience. Experience in the planning, preparation, and delivery of extemporaneous speeches will provide further guidelines for greater effectiveness in impromptu situations.

Manuscript Speeches

A manuscript speech is one that is completely written out in advance. It is used in situations where the presentation must be very precise. You would probably choose a manuscript speech if you were reporting to a group on a convention that you attended as their delegate or explaining a complicated statistical procedure. While the manuscript speech offers security to speakers afraid that they will forget what they want to say or say it badly, it has a number of disadvantages: (1) it reduces eye contact with the audience; (2) reading a speech in a spontaneous and convincing manner takes skill and practice; and (3) the speaker has difficulty in changing the language or content of a manuscript speech to adapt to the mood or reaction of the audience.

Even though you may be willing to accept these disadvantages in return for the security of a manuscript speech, the best advice is to deliver a manuscript speech only when time does not permit you to prepare and practice an extemporaneous speech or when exact word order is crucial to the success of the presentation. To deliver a manuscript speech effectively, consider the following suggestions.

1. Type your manuscript speech in capital letters, triple spaced, and underlined to ensure easy reading. Type on only one side of the paper and number the pages.

2. Edit your speech by reading each sentence aloud. Avoid overly long or complex sentences. No matter how involved or technical your material, it must be communicated clearly.

3. Indicate places of emphasis and pauses.

4. Practice your manuscript by reading it aloud at least three or four times. Become familiar enough with it so that you can maintain adequate eye contact. When possible, tape or videotape your delivery. You should sound as though you are talking to people, not reading to them.

5. Use appropriate facial expression and body action to enliven your delivery.

Memorized Speeches

A memorized speech is written out as a manuscript speech and then committed to memory. While it appears to offer the advantages of a manuscript speech along with total eye contact, it has a number of weaknesses: (1) it takes an inordinate amount of time to memorize a speech, particularly a long one; (2) it takes a skillful actor to deliver memorized material in a natural, spontaneous way; (3) the speaker who delivers a memorized speech runs the risk of forgetting; and (4) as with the manuscript speech, it is difficult to change a memorized speech to adapt to feedback from the audience. However, for the right person, the memorized speech can be an excellent method, especially for someone who plans to give the same speech a number of times.

There are times when it would be desirable to commit part of a speech to memory. You might want to memorize the first few lines of the introduction to your extemporaneous speech in order to start positively and with total eye contact. Memorizing particularly suitable words or phrases can often produce positive results. Actually, most effective speakers use a combination of different delivery methods.

Extemporaneous Speeches

Like the manuscript and memorized speech, the extemporaneous speech is carefully prepared in advance. The difference is that the speaker does not deliver the speech in a predetermined word order. Effective extemporaneous speakers usually develop their speeches in a complete sentence outline form as shown in Chapter 7. They know what they are going to say in the introduction, body, and conclusion of the speech but decide on the wording of the speech at the moment of delivery. You might compare extemporaneous speech delivery with the telling of a funny story. Most people tell a funny story extemporaneously. They are aware of the important details of the story and know how the story is going to unfold, but they haven't memorized the word order. As long as they include those details necessary to make the humor clear, they can tailor the story for any occasion. The result is a relaxed, spontaneous style, which is the main advantage of extemporaneous delivery.

Extemporaneous speakers often use note cards or an outline to help them move smoothly from one idea to the next. However, these cover the main and supporting ideas of the speech rather than the words used to express them. The extemporaneous method offers the same directness and spontaneity as the impromptu method without the danger of your rambling off the point or repeating yourself unnecessarily. For most situations, it is the most effective method of delivery.

Nonverbal Communication

In the broadest sense, nonverbal communication includes almost everything about you that communicates something to others except for the language you use. This would include the car you drive, the clothes you wear, your hairstyle, the organizations you belong to, the friends you associate with, and whatever else there is about you that communicates who you are and what you stand for. However, for the purpose of analysis we will examine only three broad areas of nonverbal communication: kinesics, paralanguage, and proxemics.

Kinesics

Kinesics is the study of how the body, face, and eyes communicate. The way you walk, your manner of gesturing, your posture, your facial expression, and the way you look at people or avoid looking at them, all say something about you to others. Whether they are interpreted by others correctly or incorrectly, these nonverbal elements communicate to others who you are.

Bodily Movement

Consider the speaker who shuffles up to the front of the room and hunches over the lectern when delivering a speech. Does that speaker's bodily movement communicate anything to you about confidence, preparation, or quality? Certainly it does. On the other hand, consider the speaker who strides briskly up to the front of the room and stands in front of the audience with good posture. Isn't that speaker saying, "Pay attention. I've got something to say to you that you will find interesting"? These two examples show the importance of positive bodily movement.

The bodily movements of your listeners can also be helpful in predicting how well you are doing in communicating. The speaker who sees audience members leaning forward in their seats knows she is doing a good job. Feedback is highly important to the communicator. You don't have to have people turn their backs to know they are not interested in what you're saying. If they lower their heads or shrug their shoulders, you soon get the idea, and if you can react to these signals and say it in another way, you will have become more aware of nonverbal audience feedback, which will improve your ability to communicate.

Another kind of bodily movement is the gesture. You can gesture with almost any part of the body. A shrug of the shoulders can communicate many things, depending on the situation. A shake of the head can indicate agreement or disagreement, depending on the direction. Toe-tapping can indicate nervousness or irritation. On the other hand, when combined with music it can also indicate that the toe-tapper is synchronized with the music. It is apparent, then, that most bodily gestures can communicate a variety of things and must be evaluated according to the situation.

Hand gestures are particularly important to the speaker. Hand gestures can be divided into two types: descriptive gestures and emphatic gestures.

Descriptive Gestures

If you are describing to your listeners how large the tomatoes you grew were or how high your fence is you can use your hands to give them an idea of shape or height. You can also use your hands to describe a winding staircase, a circle, or a square.

Another form of descriptive gesture is called the "sign." Some signs are usually instantly understandable to your audience, such as the black power sign, the "we're number one" sign, and the peace sign.

Emphatic Gestures

Emphatic gestures emphasize what you are saying. The straight arm salute accompanying "Heil Hitler" indicated the fervor the Nazis had in support of "Der Fuhrer." The synchronized gestures of cheerleaders at a pep rally emphasize the importance of the team getting out there and winning. Emphatic gestures are necessary nonverbal messages that support our concern or enthusiasm for our message. When we fail to reinforce our words with appropriate gestures we risk sending a confusing message to those with whom we are trying to communicate.

The Face and Eyes

One of the reasons for steering clear of manuscript speeches or being too dependent on notes is to avoid hiding the face and eyes, which are usually the most noticeable parts of the body. If your head is bent forward while you are speaking, your audience cannot read your facial expressions, which can communicate a range of emotions including concern, anger, happiness, enthusiasm, sadness, compassion, annoyance, and fear. Furthermore, you must look at your audience to gain feedback.

The face and eyes are also believed to contribute honesty and sincerity. Have you ever walked past someone you were angry with and diverted your glance because you didn't want to look at that person? Whether true or not, we often feel that if people don't look at us when they are telling us something important they are either lying or have something to hide.

Personal Appearance

The way you look and dress is often interpreted by others as communicating a great deal about who and what you are. Your body type, hairstyle, and the clothes you wear are perceived as variously revealing the type of personality you have, your political views, the groups you belong to, and so on. Although perceptions based solely on personal appearance can often be wrong, personal appearance is a powerful nonverbal communicator.

Body Type
In this country, people who are small boned and slender are often viewed as being meticulous, shy, sensitive, and passive; those who are large boned and plump are stereotyped as being disorganized, easygoing, jolly, and conforming; and those who are muscular and well-proportioned are seen as being rigid, extroverted, assertive, and nonconforming.

Hairstyle
The hairstyle you choose can often send strong messages to others. During the 1960s males with long hair were stereotyped by some as hippies, anti-American, and radical. In the 1980s a group of neo-Nazi "skinheads" shaved their scalps and wore Nazi emblems to identify their political affiliation. Certainly, a variety of hairstyles have emerged over the years to identify the wearer as a member of one group or another.

As we approach the twenty-first century, people seem to be less judgmental about hairstyle. Long hair, particularly if it is tastefully groomed, is considered attractive, and a shaved scalp, especially for an athlete, is considered macho. There are still some taboos, so perhaps the best advice is to avoid a far-out hairstyle or an unkempt look.

Clothing
The clothes you wear are also thought to communicate something about you. Brightly colored mod clothing tends to communicate youthfulness and energy while clothes that are more reserved in style and color (gray, brown, black) communicate age, formality, and moderation. Of course, the occasion often dictates the clothing to be worn. We wouldn't visit someone who was seriously ill wearing the casual clothes we would wear to a picnic. Similarly, the clothes you wear as a speaker should suit the occasion. For a classroom speech, wear clothing that is clean, pressed, and in good repair. For a more formal occasion, or if you want to put your best foot forward in class, wear an

appropriate dress or suit. In any event, clothing that does not call attention to itself is always the best choice.

Paralanguage

Paralanguage refers to how you say something. There are many ways that the voice can communicate. Vocal elements like rate, pause, volume, pitch, intensity, force, vocal quality, and nonfluency can either reinforce or contradict the verbal messages you are sending. Emphasizing different words within the same sentence can change the meaning of the sentence significantly. The tone of voice you use can communicate different types of emotions: anger, sadness, elation, boredom, sincerity, excitement, sarcasm, affection, fear, and so on. Like the other nonverbal elements listed above, paralanguage is of the utmost importance in communicating your meaning to others. In fact, when your voice contradicts the verbal message you are sending, most people are inclined to believe what the voice is communicating.

Vocal Elements

Rate
Rate, the speed at which a person speaks, can vary depending on the situation and the emotional attitude of the speaker. Most communication texts list the average speaking rate as between 125 to 150 words per minute. However, people who are excited, enthusiastic, or angry often speak at a much faster rate, whereas those who are lethargic, bored, or depressed speak more slowly. Because of the nonverbal connection between a faster rate and enthusiasm, announcers read hard-sell commercials considerably faster than 150 words per minute.

Pause
Pause in speech can be either filled (vocalized) or unfilled (silent). A person who pauses continuously during a speech and who fills those pauses with "ahs" and "ums" is either thought of as being nonfluent or poorly prepared. Other interpretations of this type of "filled" pause might be seen in the following examples:

1. John asks his girlfriend why she didn't call last night when she promised she would, and her explanation is replete with filled-in pauses. Rather than accepting her answer as fact, John feels she is being evasive.
2. An English professor asks one of her students to explain the difference between a restrictive and nonrestrictive clause, and the student's response is filled with "ahs" and "ums." Consequently, the professor feels the student is stalling for time or just doesn't know the answer.

Pause, however, can also be very effective. When used before an important point, pause can alert the listener to be especially attentive because something important is coming. When used at the end of an idea, it can give listeners time to think about what has been said and relate to the idea from their own experience. Effectively used, pause adds meaning and variety to a speaker's delivery.

Volume

An essential element to any communication is adequate volume—the loudness or softness of your voice. If people cannot hear you adequately, they will soon stop listening. One of the nonverbal aspects of volume is that it tends to communicate positiveness and confidence. If you asked two people the same question and one responded in a barely audible voice, while the other answered with sufficient volume, whom would you believe? Probably the second one who sounded both confident and positive—if, of course, that person did not speak too loudly. Adequate volume is essential to effective communication. However, most people view those who speak too loudly as being aggressive or boorish. Your volume will be effective if your voice can be easily heard without being offensive.

Pitch

Pitch refers to the highness or lowness of a person's voice as related to a musical scale. The length and thickness of your vocal folds determines whether your voice will be high or low. The ideal pitch level to speak at is called *optimum pitch,* which should be the pitch level most comfortable for you for speaking. One way of determining optimum pitch is to determine how low and how high you can sing, and then find the note that is one third above your lowest note. That note would be your optimum pitch. Speaking at a pitch level higher or lower than your optimum pitch can cause unpleasant quality, inadequate volume, and monotony in your speech patterns. So, if you want to avoid problems with your voice, speak at your optimum pitch level.

Inflection is the upward and downward movement of pitch. A natural conversational style is characterized by a variety of inflectional patterns. A voice without these inflectional patterns sounds monotonous and tedious. Nonverbally, upward inflectional patterns are thought to communicate enthusiasm, sincerity, and excitement while downward patterns communicate boredom, sarcasm, and dejection. To communicate enthusiasm and sincerity and to add interest to your speech, use a variety of inflectional patterns. Be aware, of course, that an overuse of upward inflection is inappropriate to serious subjects.

Quality

Your voice quality is determined by a number of things, some of which you cannot control. Two of these—timbre and resonance—are greatly influenced by the size and shape of your head and body. It is no accident that most famous opera singers have similar bodily features: wide cheekbones, large mouths, and ample lung capacity. These provide both timbre (the distinctive sound that characterizes one voice from another) and resonance (fullness and richness of sound) to their voices. However, that is not to say that without these bodily features you cannot make improvements in your vocal quality. Two well-known speech authorities, Jeffrey and Peterson, make the following suggestions for improving your vocal quality:*

> **1.** *The speaker should learn to hear his voice as others hear it. An almost universal reaction of persons upon hearing a recording of their voice for the first time is, "That's not me. There must be something wrong with the recorder." But, of course, there is nothing wrong with the recorder and the recording, as classmates or friends will verify, is a faithful reproduction of the individual's speech. The speaker's initial reaction reveals that most people do not hear themselves as others hear them. This is in part because some of the sound is carried from the voice box to his ears through the cheek and neck bones. But it is also in part because most people have become so accustomed to hearing their own voice that they really do not listen to themselves carefully or analytically.*
>
> *Quite clearly, the first step in learning to hear one's voice as others hear it is for the speaker to record and listen to his speech frequently. The second step is to develop an awareness at all times of how it sounds.*
>
> **2.** *To avoid strain, one should speak at a comfortable pitch level.*
> **3.** *The speaker should maintain adequate breath support.*
> **4.** *The speaker should remain relaxed while speaking.*
> **5.** *If strain or hoarseness occurs regularly, the speaker should consult a speech correctionist.*

Articulation

Articulation is the process of forming the consonant and vowel sounds of words. These sounds are molded into language by the five articulators: lips, teeth, tongue, hard palate, and soft palate. Improper articulation results in indistinct speech. If you articulate your words poorly, you will be difficult to understand.

Sometimes speakers are unaware that they have problems with articulation. We learn to speak by imitating the speech of those around us. Consequently, our speech habits resemble the speech habits of those we have imitated.

*Robert C. Jeffrey and Owen Peterson, *Speech: A Text with Adapted Readings* (New York: Harper & Row, Publishers, 1971), pp. 385–86.

If, for example, someone grew up in a household or neighborhood where the *d* sound was substituted for the *th* sound, that person would undoubtedly say *dis* for *this*, *doze* for *those*, and so on and perhaps not even be aware of it.

The three most common errors in articulation are running words together, substituting one sound for another, and omitting necessary sounds. For example, *did you* becomes *di ja*, *student* becomes *stoont*, *asked* becomes *ast*, and so on. This kind of careless articulation is distracting to an audience. In order to deliver your speech effectively, you must make sure that your articulation is precise.

One of the best ways to become aware of any articulation problems you might have is to record your voice with a tape recorder. Tape yourself not only while practicing your speech, but during ordinary conversation as well. Listen to your articulation carefully. What are your problems? Substituting sounds? Running words together? Omitting necessary sounds? Once you have determined your problems, you can begin working to correct them. Keep in mind though, it took you a long time to form your bad habits, so it will take time and effort to eliminate them. But rest assured, it will be time and effort well spent.

Pronunciation

While articulation is the process of forming the consonant and vowel sounds of words, pronunciation is much more complex. It involves articulating the correct consonant and vowel sounds of a word and accenting that word in a proper manner. Or put in simpler terms, pronunciation means saying a word the way it should be said. Owing to the makeup of the English language, that is not always an easy task. Several characteristics of our language make the task even harder.

First, sometimes a letter in a word is silent and should not be articulated, for instance, the *w* in *sword* and the *s* in *island*. Remember, you cannot always tell how to pronounce a word just by looking at it. When you are not sure you are saying a word correctly, consult a standard dictionary.

Second, there are an inordinate number of ways to pronounce the same vowel in our language. People who study English as a second language are often frustrated by the fact that the same vowel is often pronounced differently in different words. For example, consider the six pronunciations of the letter *o* for the following words: *do, no, dot, oar, woman,* and *women*. Even some words that are spelled alike can require different pronunciations depending on the form they take. For instance, the word *read* as in, "Read the same passage you read yesterday."

Third, correct pronunciation requires knowing how to accent words of more than one syllable. This is more difficult in some cases than in others. While the word *contact* is accented the same regardless of whether it is used as a noun, verb, adverb, or adjective, the similar word contract has the accent on the first syllable when used as a noun but on the second syllable when used as a verb. The word *rebel* is even more irregular. Not only does the accent change depending on whether the word is used as a noun or a verb but the vowel sounds change as well. Thus, the phonetic pronunciation is indicated as [reb' l] for the noun and [ri bel'] for the verb.

Finally, there are regional differences in pronunciation in the United States, called dialects. The East, the South, and the Midwest have their own dialects, and even within each region there are distinctive dialects as, for example, African American English. Because the majority of people in this country speak in a midwestern dialect, standard American dictionaries record this pronunciation. This does not, however, indicate that a midwestern dialect is superior to any other. Therefore, rather than trying to change your manner of speech, follow the best usage for your particular dialect.

Proxemics

Proxemics is the study of how space communicates nonverbally. Space can communicate all sorts of things to us. The cleric who walks down to the first row of pews to deliver a sermon is saying something different to the congregation than the one who remains behind the pulpit much farther away. The husband and wife who come to a party hand in hand and stay close to each other throughout the night are saying something different about their relationship to each other than the couple who separates when they get to the party. The African American who, years ago, had been relegated to the back of the bus, the rich family who live way up on the top of the hill, and the children who sit out in the kitchen or at a card table in another room while the parents and guests sit at the dining room table all communicate something to us about relationships.

Although in other countries the distances vary, in the United States our willingness to get close to others when communicating is directly related to the relationship we have with them. Anthropologist Edward T. Hall has identified four distances that define the type of relationship we have with the person or persons we are with.* These four distances are:

1. Intimate
2. Personal
3. Social
4. Public

*Edward Hall and Mildred Hall, "The Sounds of Silence," *Playboy,* 18 (June 1971), 148.

Intimate Distance

Intimate distance ranges from actual physical contact to eighteen inches. Usually, we only feel comfortable with this distance when we are relating to people with whom we are emotionally involved. This would usually include only a very select group: a lover, a spouse, a family member, or a dear friend. Sometimes, however, we allow even those we don't know to get this close to us; for example, hugging someone after a winning sports event or election, giving comfort to someone who has just been through a traumatic experience, or embracing another after a significant religious experience. Aside from these special situations, however, we usually feel threatened when someone invades this intimate distance; for example, we are distressed when packed together in a subway, elevator, or bus.

Personal Distance

Personal distance ranges from eighteen inches to four feet. This is the distance with which we usually feel comfortable with friends—closer with those we have established trust relationships with, and at arm's length from those we haven't yet become that close with. Unless we see someone we know as threatening, we usually feel comfortable conversing with them within this space range.

Social Distance

This third zone ranges from four to seven feet for most people and a bit farther for others. This is the space range with which most of us feel comfortable when talking in a social setting with people we have just met or when talking to a salesperson or fellow worker. Again, in this space range we feel more at ease at a closer distance with those we see as nonthreatening.

Public Distance

Public distance can range anywhere from seven to thirty feet or more. Since, as you can see, the furthest part of social distance overlaps with public distance, the situation and relationship of the communicators determines the distance. As you have seen above, some clerics communicate to their congregations from a social distance while others maintain a public distance. This is also true of teachers, some of whom lecture while sitting on their desk or standing in front of it while others stand farther away. Obviously, when speaking to a very large audience the choice is not always up to the speaker.

Exercises

Speech Assignments

1. *The impromptu speech.* Deliver a one-to-two-minute impromptu speech as your instructor directs. You will either be assigned a subject or be allowed to choose one of two drawn from a hat.

Delivery.   Keep your speech short and to the point. Make sure your purpose and central idea are clear to your audience.

Sample Topics

1. The perfect age
2. My favorite teacher
3. The ideal husband (wife)
4. What I like (hate) about my job
5. Why _____ should be legalized
6. How to bounce a meatball

2. *A speech of criticism.* Deliver a two-to-three-minute speech criticizing a person, policy, or organization. Express your views in a direct, to-the-point manner, emphasizing your annoyance with the language you choose.

Delivery.   This is an expression of viewpoint. You are not attempting to persuade someone to agree with you. Communicate your annoyance with appropriate gesture, facial expression, and tone of voice.

Sample Topics

1. Star Wars is stupidity.
2. Abortion is murder.
3. My cousin is an idiot.
4. Our prison system is cruel and inhuman.
5. Welfare is another word for stealing.

The speech evaluation form shown in Figure 9-1 is designed for both student and instructor evaluation. It lists those characteristics of content and delivery that should be considered when evaluating a speaker.

The student evaluation form shown in Figure 9-2 is designed for critiquing the speeches of classmates, and for providing a comprehensive list of desirable speech characteristics for self-evaluation and for judging speeches outside of the speech class.

	Poor --	1	2	3	4	--Excellent	Comments
A. Delivery							
1. Appearance							
2. Bodily Movement							
3. Directness							
4. Gesture							
B. Voice							
1. Rate/Pause							
2. Volume/Tone							
3. Pitch/Inflection							
4. Articulation Pronunciation							
C. Content							
1. Subject							
2. Preparation							
3. Supports							
4. Language							
D. Organization							
1. Introduction							
2. Transitions							
3. Body							
4. Conclusion							

FIGURE 9-1 Speech Evaluation Form

Speaker _____ Speech # _____ Date _____

Subject _____ Purpose _____

Delivery	Organization
____ Dresses appropriately	____ Begins with attention step
____ Manner relaxed—confident	____ Central idea introduced
____ Maintains good posture	____ Need step used if appropriate
____ Steps up briskly	____ Body of speech previewed
____ Moves with confidence	____ Transitions provide coherence
____ Effective facial expression	____ Body has 2–5 main points
____ Focuses on audience	____ Main points follow pattern
____ Uses notes unobtrusively	____ Supporting points clear
____ Good eye contact	____ Conclusion provides review
____ Gestures meaningfully	____ Conclusion closes effectively
____ Gestures emphatically	____ Conclusion reinforces thesis
____ Handles aids effectively	____ Time limit followed

Voice	Content
____ Rate appropriate to topic	____ Subject interesting, appropriate
____ Rate varied effectively	____ Purpose clear
____ Pause added variety	____ Speaker demonstrates know-ledge
____ Pause added emphasis	
____ Volume varied effectively	____ Speech adapted to audience
____ Volume added emphasis	____ Examples clear and relevant
____ Tone quality appropriate	____ Statistics documented
____ Pitch level comfortable	____ Explanations clear
____ Inflection varied	____ Comparisons effective
____ Delivery conversational	____ Testimony authoritative
____ Articulation distinct	____ Supports effectively combined
____ Pronunciation correct	____ Language clear, concise
	____ Language appropriate

Comments/Suggestions

FIGURE 9-2   Student Evaluation Form

10

Informing

We live in an increasingly complex age—one of new technology, endless research, and specialization. Each year more and more new information is added to the total of human knowledge in our world. It is estimated that by the year 2000 there will be 1,000 times more knowledge in the world than there was in 1900. It is obvious, then, how important it is for us to be able to send and receive informative communication accurately and effectively.

All too often we take informative communication for granted. We listen to weather forecasts, news stories, stock market updates, and traffic reports with only half an ear and then wonder why we didn't get things straight. We give vague instructions as to where and when we're going to meet someone or exactly how we'd like our hair done and then become irritated when things go wrong. The purpose of informative communication is to add to a listener's understanding. In order to achieve this goal a speaker must communicate information clearly and interestingly.

There are many different ways to categorize informative speeches. This chapter will deal with four of the most popular categories: demonstration speeches, definition speeches, description speeches, and exposition speeches.

Demonstration Speeches

The informative demonstration speech is designed to show your audience how to do something so that they will be able to do it on their own or have a better understanding of how it is done. Thus, you might deliver a demonstration speech to teach your audience how to make Swedish pancakes or to show them how various mathematical problems can be solved with a slide rule. As with most speeches, the key to delivering a demonstration speech successfully is effective audience analysis. You must ask the question, "What response can I reasonably expect from my listeners?" You could teach an audience to make Swedish pancakes in a reasonable amount of time; however, unless those in your audience were familiar with a slide rule, it seems unlikely that you could do much more than give them an understanding of how a slide rule can be used.

In order to show someone how to perform a card trick, prepare a salad, carve a turkey, or read palms you will want to use the technique of demonstration. Demonstration speeches can either involve participation from the audience or can be nonparticipative. In demonstrating the card trick, for example, you might ask one or two members of the audience to try the trick to show how easily it can be learned. When demonstrating palm reading, you might have members of your audience read the lines and marks on their own palms to identify their life lines, their character, and so on. When members of your audience are observers rather than participants in your demonstration, you must be careful to present your material clearly and interestingly enough so that you achieve your purpose: audience understanding.

Following are examples of demonstration speeches:

Demonstrations to Teach	*Demonstrations for Understanding*
How to:	How:
wrap a gift	a parachute is packed
recognize cuts of beef	a head is shrunk
apply a tourniquet	belly dancing is done
remove a stain	a lute is played
cover a book	a person is hypnotized
give a facial	fires get started
take good snapshots	an abacus is used
toss a salad	ballet is danced

Listed below are eight suggestions for making your demonstration speeches clear and interesting.

1. Practice your speech exactly as you plan to deliver it. If you are showing how to make a tossed salad, mix the ingredients in practice just as you would in front of an audience. This will enable you to time your speech accurately. (It might take you longer to prepare and toss the ingredients than you thought it would.)

2. Determine whether the audience will see the usefulness of your demonstration. If it is not obvious to your audience that they have something to gain from paying attention to your demonstration, tell why your information will be useful to them during your introduction.

3. Break your speech down into units or steps so that it can be more easily followed by your audience.

4. Preview the steps you are going to follow in your introduction and summarize them in your conclusion. If your demonstration is long or complicated, consider a review of what has been said during the body of your speech.

5. Provide continuity to your discussion by talking throughout. Don't be like one young student who began her speech by saying, "Today I'm going to show you how to make Swedish meatballs," and then proceeded to make them without saying another word for the next three minutes. Her meatballs were excellent; her speech was not.

6. Make sure that what you are showing the audience can easily be seen by all. Keep in mind that you must reach the entire audience, not just those in front. If you are not sure your demonstration can easily be seen, estimate the distance from your farthest listener and have a friend take a similar position to check visibility.

7. Maintain your cool. If you make a mistake, acknowledge it and go on. Your audience will appreciate the fact that you admitted your error.

8. Conform to a predetermined time limit for your speech. Before your speech you decided what you wanted to show your audience and how much time you wanted to spend doing it. Don't change that during your delivery.

Definition Speeches

A definition speech can often be an effective classroom assignment. A speech on what you consider to be the "ideal wife" or "husband" can give your audience insights as to the kind of person you are and allow you to share with them your feelings about the type of person you see as the ideal spouse. Defining other broadly abstract terms like "democracy," "truth," or "beauty" can be a challenging and rewarding exercise.

The primary purpose of informative communication is to be understood. This is unlikely to happen if you use abstract language or language with which your audience is unfamiliar. In situations, however, where you must use words that are unfamiliar to your audience, be sure to define the words before using them. This is especially important when using technical terms you will be repeating in your speech. Don't avoid using an unfamiliar technical term—just explain the term the moment you use it. Your definitions can be either short or long and stated in your own words or the words of someone else. Avoid using dictionary or overly complicated definitions that are difficult to understand. Remember, your goal is to be understood but also interesting. Following are samples of definition speeches:

1. Omnicide: The End of Humanity
2. The Autistic Child

3. What Is "Child Abuse"?
4. The Star Wars Myth
5. The Ideal Marriage
6. What Is "Integrity"?
7. Is America a Free Country?
8. AIDS: A Killer Disease

Using definition as a part of a longer speech is also often necessary. Few words in the English language are more familiar to us then the word "love." Yet, perhaps no other word in our language is more abstract. It has a different meaning for almost anyone. Any speaker delivering a speech on love would have to give an extended definition of love in order to ensure audience understanding.

In a sermon delivered at the Dexter Avenue Baptist Church in Montgomery, Alabama, on Christmas 1957, the Reverend Martin Luther King, Jr., used the following examples to make clear to his audience exactly what he meant when he spoke of love:

> *The meaning of love is not to be confused with some sentimental outpouring. Love is something much deeper than sentimental bosh. Perhaps the Greek language can clear our confusion at this point. In the Greek New Testament are three words for love. The word* eros *is a sort of aesthetic or romantic love. In the Platonic dialogues eros is a yearning of the soul for the realm of the divine. The second word is* philia, *a reciprocal love and the intimate affection and friendship between friends. We love those whom we like, and we love because we are loved. The third word is* agape, *understanding and creative, redemptive goodwill for all men. An overflowing love which seeks nothing in return, agape is the love of God operating in the human heart. At this level, we love men not because we like them, nor because their ways appeal to us, nor even because they possess some type of divine spark; we love every man because God loves him. At this level, we love the person who does an evil deed, although we hate the deed he does.*

As you can see, Dr. King used a number of devices for defining love, including example, comparison/contrast, etymology, and detail. Below are specific suggestions for using these devices to make your definition speeches and definitions clear and interesting to your listeners.

Define by Example

This type of definition involves using detailed or undetailed examples to clarify a word or concept. It is especially useful when dealing with the abstract. For example, the concept "neighbor" is decidedly abstract. Who is your neighbor—the person next door, a person in the same town, a fellow American, or a starving child in a Third World country? If you used the term in a speech, you would want to be sure that your listeners had a clear understanding of exactly what you meant when you used it. An excellent instance of how a detailed example provides an understanding of the concept "neighbor" is the parable of the Good Samaritan, found in the tenth chapter of Luke in the Holy Bible. In response to the question, "Who is my neighbor?" Jesus replies:

> *A certain man was going down from Jerusalem to Jericho when robbers attacked him, stripped him and beat him up leaving him half dead. It so happened that a priest was going down the road; when he saw the man he walked on by, on the other side. In the same way a Levite also came there, went over and looked at the man, and then walked on by, but a certain Samaritan who was traveling that way looked upon him, and when he saw the man his heart was filled with pity. He walked over to him, poured oil and wine on his wounds and bandaged them; then he put the man on his own animal and took him to an inn where he took care of him. The next day he took out two silver coins and gave them to the innkeeper. "Take care of him," he told the innkeeper, "and when I come back this way again, I will pay you back whatever you spend on him." And Jesus concluded, which one of these three seems to you to have been a neighbor to the man attacked by the robbers?**

Define by Comparison or Contrast

An effective way of defining something unknown to your audience is by comparing it or contrasting it to something that is known. In Sonnet 18, William Shakespeare uses comparison to clearly define the one he loves.

> Shall I compare thee to a summer's day?
> Thou art more lovely and more temperate:
> Rough winds do shake the darling buds of May,
> And summer's lease hath all too short a date;
> Sometime too hot the eye of heaven shines,
> And often is his gold complexion dimm'd,
> And every fair from fair sometime declines,
> By chance or nature's changing course untrimm'd:
> But thy eternal summer shall not fade,
> Nor lose possession of that fair thou ow'st,
> Nor shall Death brag thou wand'rest in his shade,

*From *Today's English Version of the New Testament.* Copyright © American Bible Society, 1966, 1971.

When in eternal lines to time thou grow'st.
So long as men can breathe or eyes can see,
So long lives this, and this gives life to thee.

Define by Etymology

As you know, one of the reasons that English is such a difficult language to communicate with is that many of the words we use came from other languages. Etymology refers to how and where a word originated and how it relates to other words in the language. Sometimes a word can be better understood if you explain its "root" to your audience. For example, the word *genocide,* which originated during World War II as a result of the Nazis' attempt to exterminate the Jews, comes from the Greek *genus,* meaning "race," and the French *cide,* meaning "killing."

Define by Details

Another method for defining abstract or complex terms is to discuss them in detail. Sometimes when you examine the parts of a picture, you get a better understanding of it as a whole. In the following example the author provides her audience with details to give them a clear understanding of how difficult survival is for children and senior citizens of the Ilk Tribe in the African country Uganda:

> *The Ilks turn their children out of the house when they are about three years of age. Parents make their children sleep in the open, providing their own shelter. The younger children of the tribe band together for protection against both the elements and older children. Even when the children fight viciously among themselves, the adults do not interfere. As a result, only the strongest children survive to take their places in adult society. This harsh treatment has purpose, because the Ilk consider children to be useless, expendable burdens, just as they do the aged. Adults are as cruel and neglectful of their elders as they are of their young children. Ilk elders who become sick and infirm are not fed or nurtured, but are simply allowed to fend for themselves or die.**

Define with Sensory Aids

Can you imagine trying to explain the difference between country rock and acid rock without having your audience listen to an example of each? Try to describe orally the sound of a flute or synthesizer or the cry of a loon. Con-

---

*Grace J. Craig, *Human Development,* 2nd ed. (Englewood Cliffs, NJ: Prentice-Hall, 1980), pp. 10–11.

sider explaining the colors puce or magenta. The dictionary defines puce as brownish purple and magenta as purplish red. Does that give you a clear picture? Probably not. Have you ever prepared a meal of liver and onions? What does the liver feel like as you are cutting it? What does it smell like when it is frying? What does it taste like when you eat it?

In some cases an oral explanation might be largely meaningless unless your audience also sensually experiences the concept you are explaining. When delivering a demonstration speech that will be enhanced by the use of a sensory aid, use one. For example, if you are going to show your audience how to make brownies, bake a batch the night before and pass them out so they can taste the finished product.

Description Speeches

A third method of communicating information, description, makes use of sensory appeals to give the listener a clear picture of what is being communicated. In a description speech you describe an object, person, place, event, or experience. You might give your listeners information about an object's appearance, what it sounds like, what it tastes like, what it feels like, or what it smells like. You might describe a major event that you witnessed and what it felt like to be there. The key to effective description is accurate, specific detail. The more accurate and specific your details are, the more likely it will be that your listeners will be able to get a clear picture of what you are describing. Note how in the following excerpt the writer uses specific detail to give his audience a clear picture of the city of Las Vegas.

> *It's a 24-hour figment of some surreal imagination, a jerry-built collection of neon rising out of the red desert sand.*
>
> *Covered with sagebrush and tumbleweed, and decorated with several billion dollars' worth of glass, plastic, steel and concrete—Las Vegas transcends the normal definitions of reality.*
>
> *It is a town of high heels and sneakers, designer jeans and Levi's, gold neck chains and pale-green polyester leisure suits.*
>
> *It's a town where absolute strangers can meet at a bubbling fountain of free champagne, exchange life histories while filling their glasses, and depart, each knowing that neither will have to prove the truth of anything said to the other.*
>
> *They treat $100 bills like matchsticks here, but you can still make a public telephone call for a dime. Thirty-year-old blackjack dealers here have 50-year-old eyes. And 70-year-old hands.*
>
> *You can get a bacon, egg, toast and hashbrown breakfast at dinnertime for 99 cents, or a New York strip steak breakfast for $2.95. And you can*

catch a glimpse of Sinatra at Caesar's Palace, after a 2-hour wait, for $40—
cocktails at $3.50 each, extra.

This is a city of 6-foot showgirls not counting the feathers, of lavish and
elaborate musical stage productions, of real celebrities doing real things like
waiting for elevators.

It is a town of 24-hour wedding chapels where there is no waiting
period, and no blood test required; where marriage licenses may be obtained
any time between 8 a.m. Friday and midnight Sunday, and between 8 a.m.
and midnight any other day; and where almost 58,000 people were married
last year, and where 9,000 were divorced.

It is a city where a blissful couple, heedless of the 40-degree midnight
temperature, can be found in their bathing suits sipping cocktails and
dangling their legs in the heated waters of the hotel's outdoor swimming
pool.*

Types of Description Speeches

Descriptions of people, places, and events are part of our everyday communication. We insist on an in-depth description of our roommate's cousin
before agreeing to a blind date. We talk to a number of people who have vaca-
tioned at that new island paradise before we agree to go. We listen to a
description of the events that took place at last year's homecoming game
before buying our tickets for this year's game. Following are five types of
descriptive speeches:

Introducing Yourself
Perhaps one of the first speeches you will be asked to deliver is one in which
you introduce yourself to the rest of the class. Since you should be an authority on yourself, the content of this speech should pose no problem for you.
Include those things that you feel will be of interest to the class.

Introducing a Classmate
Another type of introductory speech involves describing a classmate to your
audience. Describe his or her accomplishments, talents, hobbies, goals, likes
and dislikes, or anything you think will be of interest to the class.

Describing a Place
A vivid description of your hometown or favorite place can make an effective
speech. This can be a particularly effective presentation when the speaker is
describing a location with which most of the audience is unfamiliar.

---

*Donald A. Bluhm, *Milwaukee Journal,* March 20, 1983. Reprinted by permission.

Describing an Event

The description of an event can be an effective informatory speech. An eye-witness account of the Olympic Games, a rocket launching, a bank robbery, or other such topics could be developed into exciting, attention-holding presentations.

Describing Historical Events

The historical events speech involves describing an episode or sequence of events in history. A vivid description of the scene, characters, and setting of the battle of the Alamo would effectively hold an audience's attention. Following are samples of historical events speeches:

The Battle of Bunker Hill	Custer's Last Stand
Watergate	The Exodus
D-Day	The Valentine's Day Massacre

While description is a technique that can be used in any of the other kinds of speeches, sometimes it is necessary to develop an entire speech of description. If you want your listeners to have a greater appreciation for a classmate, for example, you might describe her accomplishments, talents, goal, hobbies, and likes and dislikes. Listed below are samples of speeches of description:

1. Summerfest in Milwaukee
2. Superbowl 1998: The Perfect Matchup
3. Carol Marking: The Ideal Classmate
4. Copenhagen: The Perfect Vacation Spot
5. Abraham Lincoln: Our Greatest President
6. The Duckbill Platypus
7. Life in a Dormitory
8. Las Vegas: City of Dreams

Exposition Speeches

The primary purpose of exposition is to inform. It is communication that explains a concept, process, idea, or belief. It can include explanation, analysis, comparison/contrast, and example.

Types of Expository Speeches

Expository speeches are those which explain a process, concept, idea, or belief. They include speeches to explain a process, to instruct, and to review.

Speeches to Explain a Process

Speeches to explain a process inform an audience how something works. While they are often organized similarly to demonstration speeches, they differ in purpose. A student studying photography might deliver a demonstration speech on how to take an effective snapshot. If he or she is asked to deliver an explain-a-process speech, an appropriate choice would be: how a camera works. Following are examples of explain-a-process speeches.

How:

a generator works	a microlaser operates
food is digested	a steam engine works
photosynthesis occurs	Project Elf functions
the eye functions	kidneys clean your blood

Speeches to Instruct

Instructive speeches are presentations in which the speaker gives facts and information about concepts or ideas. The topic of a typical instructive speech would be: what makes the sky blue? These speeches can be thought of as informal class lectures. In order to deliver an instructive speech effectively, you should try to choose a subject that will be either useful or interesting to your listeners. Following are samples of instructive speeches:

Ideas of Thoreau	Solar energy
The chromatic scale	What controls the tide?
Nuclear submarines	Supply-side economics

Book Reviews

Reviews of current novels, television shows, short stories, or plays can provide effective material for an informative speech. Choose one that you feel you are qualified to analyze and that will be interesting to your listeners.

Speeches of exposition may include elements of demonstration, definition, or description speeches. For example, in speaking of solar energy you will need to define exactly what it is and describe how it works. However, expository speeches rely largely on explanation, analysis, comparison/contrast, and example.

Explanation

A significant form of exposition is the explanation. The primary purpose of explanation is to make things clear or understandable. As a student, you are constantly involved with explanations. The school bulletin explains what courses your school offers and which ones you have to take to satisfy the requirements for your degree. Your instructors and advisors are primarily explainers. The syllabi you get at the beginning of the semester are explanations of what you will be studying in each course and what you are expected to accomplish.

The first rule to follow when you are going to use explanation is that you must thoroughly understand something before you can explain it to someone else. A second rule is always to use words in your explanation that will be clear to your audience. To use technical terms to explain a process or concept with which your audience is unfamiliar will be self-defeating. Note how Malcolm X uses references common to the experiences of his audience to explain what revolution is and is not:

> *This is a real revolution. Revolution is always based on land. Revolution is never based on begging someone for an integrated cup of coffee. Revolutions are never based upon love-your-enemy and pray-for-those-who-spitefully-use-you. And revolutions are never waged singing "We shall Overcome." Revolutions are based upon bloodshed. Revolutions are never compromising. Revolutions are never based upon any kind of tokenism whatsoever. Revolutions overturn systems. And there is no system which has proven itself more corrupt, more criminal, than this system that in 1964 still colonizes 22 million African-Americans, still enslaves 22 million Afro-Americans.**

Analysis

Analysis involves breaking down a situation or concept into its parts in order to examine each part separately. It often asks such questions as, Who? What? Why? When? Where? How? It is used frequently in speeches to inform. When organizing a speech titled "How Our Government Operates," you might divide your speech into three parts: (1) the legislative, (2) the executive, and (3) the judicial, and examine each branch separately.

The following excerpt from a TV speech delivered by President John F. Kennedy on October 22, 1962 uses analysis to show how our country was threatened by the Cuban missile sites:

> *This government as promised has maintained the closest surveillance of the Soviet military build-up on the island of Cuba. Within the past week unmistakable evidence has established the fact that a series of offensive missile sites is now in preparation on that imprisoned island. The purpose of these bases can be none other than to provide a nuclear strike capability against the Western Hemisphere.*

The characteristics of these new missile sites indicate two distinct types of installations. Several of them include medium-range ballistic missiles capable of carrying a nuclear warhead for a distance of more than 1,000 nautical miles. Each of these missiles, in short, is capable of striking Washington, D.C., the Panama Canal, Cape Canaveral, Mexico City, or any other city in the southeastern part of the United States, in Central America, or in the Caribbean area.

Additional sites not yet completed appear to be designed for intermediate-range missiles capable of traveling more than twice as far, and thus capable of striking most of the major cities in the Western Hemisphere. This urgent transformation of Cuba into an important strategic base by the presence of these large long-range and clearly offensive weapons of sudden mass destruction constitutes an explicit threat to the peace and security of all the Americas.*

Explication

Explication is a form of analysis that makes clear what is obscure or implied. Often in this form of analysis you will want to use the testimony of experts to back up the information you are giving your listeners. Thus, in a speech titled "The Fallout Dangers of Star Wars," a student speaker quotes a noted authority to back up her thesis that "radioactive fallout from the proposed Star Wars system would probably devastate our environment and the entire human race":

According to Dr. E. J. Sternglass, professor emeritus of radiological physics at the University of Pittsburgh School of Medicine, "A technologically perfect missile shield that is capable of intercepting every incoming nuclear warhead would in all probability still fail to protect the U.S. No shield, no matter how effective, would prevent radioactive fallout produced in space from damaging all living things on our planet. Not only would bombs exploded in space drop radioactivity on earth—but the defense system itself could add to the fallout."†

Evaluation

Evaluation is another form of analysis. Perhaps, as a student, you have already been asked to give an end-of-the-course evaluation, or in the future you will have to evaluate a teacher, or the school, or yourself. When you use this technique, keep in mind that in order to be informative, evaluations must be objective. That is not always easy.

Reviews are a form of evaluation. Many of us listen to reviews on the radio or TV to decide which movies or programs we will watch or at which

---

*Vital Speeches 26 (November 15, 1962), 66.
†With permission of the speaker, Carol Marking.

restaurants we will dine. Following is a student newspaper review of the CD
Recycler, by the rock group ZZ Top:

> *It's been five years since* ZZ Top *released its last CD,* Afterburner, *so the
> arrival of its latest,* Recycler (WEA), *is a welcoming of blues-influenced
> rock'n'roll.*
>
> *During its hiatus between efforts, the group has been involved with the*
> Delta City Blues Museum. *This relationship has influenced the Top here
> more than one would ever imagine. Yes, it's still Texas boogie, but on this
> effort the emphasis is back to the band's blues roots.*
>
> *You know how* Living Color *has that great metal sound with that fat
> funk underlining? Reverse that combination and you know* Tack Head
> (SBK) *and its latest* Strange Things, *a sure-fire way to heat up these win-
> ter nights.*
>
> *On this self-produced effort the band has a lot to say about our society,
> but most impressive is the way it presents its message musically. Enticing
> musical chops abound on this, the group's second release. Performed and
> sampled funk with some original slashing guitar solos are splashed through-
> out this 11-track CD.*
>
> *Standouts include "Nobody to Somebody," "Take a Stroll" (with* Mick
> Jagger *on harmonica), "See the Fire Burning" (with* Melle Mel), *and
> "Dangerous Sex."**

Comparison/Contrast

As you have seen above, comparison/contrast is the act of examining two or
more things in order to determine differences or similarities. A fundamental
principle of education is that the only way you can teach anything to students
is to relate it to what they already know. Comparing the ideas that you are presenting to concepts that your listeners can relate to from their own experiences
will improve your chances of success. In the following excerpt the author
gives his reader a clearer understanding of the writing process by comparing
it to building a wall:

> *In northern New England, where I live, stone walls mark boundaries, bor-
> der meadows, and march through the woods that grew up around them long
> ago. Flank-high, the walls are made of granite rocks stripped from fields
> when pastures were cleared and used to fence in cattle. These are dry walls
> made without mortar, and the stones in them, all shapes and sizes, are fitted
> to one another with such care that a wall, built a hundred years ago, still
> runs as straight and solid as it did when people cleared the land.*

*By Duane Rodriguez. With permission of the *MATC Times.* From the November 20, 1990, issue
of the *Times.*

Writing is much like wall-building. The writer fits together separate chunks of meaning to make an understandable statement. Like the Old Yankee wall-builders, anyone who wants to write well must learn some basic skills, one at a time, to build soundly.*

Example

The use of detailed or undetailed examples can be a clear and interesting way to present information. Biographies and autobiographies are written to give us information about a person's life. When your grandparents tell you what life was like when they were your age, they are using examples to inform. A series of examples can be an excellent way of introducing a speech. The amount of detail to include in your examples is dependent on your listeners. If you feel your listeners are unfamiliar with your example, you must develop it in detail. If the example you are using is familiar to your listener you need only cite it briefly. Examples that are both interesting and relevant are bound to ensure both attention and understanding.

For example, in an 1866 speech to a group of English workingmen, Thomas Huxley, a renowned biologist, explained the process of induction in terms that were familiar to those in his audience. Here is an updated paraphrase of the speech Huxley delivered over 130 years ago:

Suppose you go into a fruit shop wanting an apple—you take one up and upon biting it you find that it is sour. You look at it and see that it is hard and green. You take another one and that too is hard, green, and sour. The shopkeeper offers you a third, but before biting it you examine it and find that it is hard and green, and you immediately say that you don't want it since it must be sour like those you have already tried.

Nothing can be more simple than that, you think; but if you will take the trouble to analyze and trace out into its logical elements what has been done by the mind, you will be greatly surprised. In the first place, you will have performed the process of induction. You found that in two experiences, hardness and greenness in apples went together with sourness. You found a general law, that all hard and green apples are sour; and that, as far as it goes, is a perfect induction.

Guidelines for Informative Speaking

To communicate effectively, you must have the attention of your audience. In fact, without attention communication does not exist. Listeners will not pay

---

*Roger Garrison, *How a Writer Works* (New York: Harper & Row, Publishers, 1981), p. 4.

attention for long to a speech that is neither clear nor interesting. Below are specific suggestions:

Make Your Material Clear

The purpose of informative speaking is to add to a listener's understanding. In order to do this a speaker must communicate clearly. You can help make your material clear by using words that are familiar and specific and by using descriptive gestures.

Use Familiar Words

Be assured, unless your listener understands the message, communication will not take place. Sometimes speakers are so concerned with impressing their audience with their vocabularies that they actually fail to communicate. This can be a serious mistake. Unlike the reader who can reread an unclear passage or look up unfamiliar words, the listener misses part of the message unless the words the speaker uses are understood instantly. Therefore, when you choose your words as a speaker, always choose those that are the most familiar. For example, why say fecund instead of fertile, efficacious rather than effective, and so on? If you want everyone in your audience to understand you, use terms that are familiar to them.

In situations, however, where you must use words that are unfamiliar to your audience be sure to define the words before using them. This is especially important when using technical terms that you will be repeating in your speech. Don't avoid using an unfamiliar technical term—just explain the term the moment you use it.

Use Specific Words

An effective way of making your ideas clear to others is to use specific language. To say that a person entered the room gives your listener little information. To say that he or she strutted, ambled, staggered, crept, or marched says it more clearly. The word *tree* is general. *Fruit tree* is more specific. But *Bartlett pear, Courtland apple,* and *Bing cherry* are much more specific and therefore much clearer.

Sometimes a difficult concept can be made clear by explaining it in specific terms. Many people, for example, are unaware of the danger involved in improper disposal of nuclear waste. The student who began her speech, "Even though the dosages would be microscopic so that you couldn't even see them, if two pounds of plutonium could be evenly distributed among the world's population, each person on earth would receive a lethal dosage," used the specific to give her audience a better understanding as to the magnitude of the problem.

Use Descriptive Gestures

Descriptive gestures aid by giving your audience a clearer picture of something. You might gesture to show your audience a proper golf swing or to give them an idea of the size of the tomatoes you grew. Or you might give your audience a clear picture of how effective karate can be for self-defense by demonstrating different karate techniques with a volunteer. Descriptive gestures not only make your ideas clearer, they also aid in maintaining audience interest.

Make Your Material Interesting

You must have the attention of your listeners if you want to communicate anything to them. Emphasis and variety will help to hold their attention by making your material as interesting as possible.

Emphasis

We emphasize our ideas in speech nonverbally and verbally. An upward inflection and an increase in volume often indicate great enthusiasm. You can tell when people are concerned by the intensity with which they say things. Tone of voice can emphasize, as can pause. Used before an important idea, pause says to an audience, "Pay close attention to what is coming next." A pause after an idea sets the idea apart and gives each listener a chance to reflect on what was said.

Besides being descriptive, gestures also emphasize. A positive movement of the hands or arms or a nod of the head may emphasize an idea or a point you are making. Leaning or moving toward your audience suggests interest or emphasis. Remember, gestures must be seen to be effective. A good rule of thumb is the larger the audience, the broader the gesture.

Another way to emphasize your ideas is to preview and summarize them. List the points you are going to make or steps you are going to follow in your introduction and summarize them in your conclusion.

Variety

Most of us prefer to listen to a speaker with a pleasant, conversational style, one who seems to talk with you rather than to you. The key to the conversational style is speaking in a natural manner. In everyday conversation people speak with various vocal patterns to indicate the meanings they wish to convey. Their voices rise and fall as they inflect from one pitch to another, their volume increases or decreases depending upon their subject and how they feel about it, and their rate varies anywhere from 90 words a minute to over 180.

However, put many of these same people in a public speaking situation and they become overly aware that some are forming opinions about what they say and the way they are saying it. They become conscious of how they look and sound and what they are saying. The result is that they lose their naturalness and spontaneity. They convey words (rather than meaning) in a flat, colorless way.

The next time you are engaged in enthusiastic conversation with your friends, make note of their speech patterns, gestures, and facial expressions. Yours will be similar. If you can transfer your animation and physical expression in informal conversation to public speaking, you will be more interesting and enjoyable to listen to and watch.

Sample Full-Sentence Outline for a Speech to Instruct

Below is a sample complete-sentence outline of a speech to instruct on the contributions African Americans have made to this country.

Black Is Beautiful

Introduction

I. Did you know that there were more than 5,000 African American cowboys in the Old West, and that an African American named Bill Pickett invented the technique of "bulldogging?" Are you aware that African American participation in the development of this country began in the early 1600s? (Attention getters)

II. I learned quite a few interesting facts like these when I attended a series of lectures on campus during Black History week last semester. Since then, I've been reading a lot and browsing the Internet learning about African American heroes. (Indicate qualifications)

III. I learned that African Americans have contributed significantly to this nation's development. (Central idea statement) I was amazed, though somewhat disappointed, that I hadn't heard these things before.

IV. The record shows that African American men and women have been in the forefront of our progress as a nation throughout the years. These are things everyone should know about American history. (Reason for listening)

V. That's why I'm going to tell you about some famous African Americans and also about some lesser-known African Americans who have contributed to our growth, have been dedicated to our welfare, and have added to the quality of life here in this land of ours (Preview statement)

Body

I. Throughout our history, African American men and women have contributed significantly to the growth of the United States.

   A. African Americans were instrumental in developing this country.

      1. African Americans sailed with Columbus on his voyages to the New World.

      2. African Americans were with Coronado in New Mexico and de Soto in Alabama.

      3. York, an African American slave, traveled with Lewis & Clark on their Northwest Passage to the Pacific.

      4. Jean Baptise Dusable, an African American, founded Chicago.

   B. African Americans have furthered industrial expansion in the United States. Four significant contributions were:

      1. Lewis Latimer invented the first long-lasting lightbulb and the safety elevator.

      2. Granville T. Woods invented the third rail.

      3. Garrett Augustus Morgen invented the gas mask.

      4. Shelby J. Davidson invented the adding machine.

II. Over the years, African Americans have been dedicated to the welfare of the United States.

   A. African Americans have served illustriously in defending our country.

      1. Over 5,000 African Americans served in the Continental Army.

      2. African Americans fought with valor in the War of 1812.

      3. In World War I, 370,000 African Americans served their country with valor.

         a. The 369th received more citations than any other regiment.

         b. The 369th, 370th, and, 371st were awarded France's highest honor.

      4. Over one million African Americans enlisted in World War II.

         a. The all-African American Panther tank battalion overwhelmed the Nazis.

         b. Benjamin O. Davis became the nation's first African American general.

   B. African American religious and political leaders have enriched our values.

      1. Frederick Douglas worked with and influenced eight presidents.

      2. Reverend Martin Luther King, Jr., stirred America's soul with his dream of equality for all.

3. Shirley Chisolm became the first African American woman to be elected to Congress, fought tirelessly for the rights of the disenfranchised.

4. Reverend Jesse Jackson has been an outspoken advocate of social, political, and economic justice for all.

C. African Americans have contributed significantly in the field of medicine.

1. Dr. Daniel Hale Williams performed America's first open-heart operation.

2. George Washington Carver found over four-hundred uses for the peanut and sweet potato.

3. Dr. Benjamin Carsen was the first neurosurgeon to separate Siamese twins joined at the head.

4. Dr. Charles Drew, and expert on blood plasma, set up the first blood bank.

III. From the outset, African Americans have contributed to the quality of life in our country.

A. African American contributions to the cultural arts have been impressive.

1. Marion Anderson, the first African American to sing at the Metropolitan Opera, won the National Medal of Arts.

2. Alex Haley was awarded the Pulitzer Prize for his novel, *Roots*.

3. Sydney Poitier won the Academy Award for his performance in *Lilies of the Field.*

4. Maya Angelou, author of *I Know Why the Caged Bird Sings,* was awarded the National Book Award.

B. African Americans have excelled in the area of sports.

1. Jack Johnson won the world heavyweight boxing championship in 1903.

2. Jesse Owens was the first athlete to win four gold medals in the Olympics.

3. Hank Aaron set a new world record with 755 home runs.

4. Jackie Joyner-Kersee was declared world's greatest female athlete after winning six medals at the 1988 Olympics.

C. African American entertainers have shown remarkable talent.

1. Harry Belafonte—world renowned singer—has won two Emmy Awards.

2. Cicely Tyson won Best Actress of the Year for her role in *The Auto-biography of Miss Jane Pittman.*
3. Bill Cosby was named the entertainer of the Twentieth Century.
4. Denzel Washington, a matinee idol of the 1990s, won an Academy Award for his performance in the Civil War film *Glory.*

Conclusion

I. This nation owes a debt of gratitude to African Americans who have helped to develop and defend this country, have been dedicated to its welfare, and have added to the quality of life of its citizens. (Summary of main points)

II. African Americans have made significant inroads in the field of medicine, impressive contributions in fine arts, sports, and entertainment; and have enriched our values.

III. Many African American actors, musicians, and writers are world renowned. It is easy to see why the words *Black* and *beautiful* are synonymous.

IV. I hope I have introduced you to some African American heroes you hadn't heard of and that you now have a better understanding of how different people in this country have worked together for the common good. The Reverend Martin Luther King, Jr., said that understanding and creative goodwill for all comes from the love of God operating in the human heart. "We love men," he said, "not because we like them, nor because their ways appeal to us, nor even because they possess some type of divine spark; we love every man because God loves him."

Bibliography
Abdul-Jabbar, Kareem. *Black Profiles in Courage.* New York: William Morrow, 1996.
Brier, Steven, et al. *Who Built America?* Pantheon Books, 1992.
Brodie, James. *Created Equal: The Lives and Ideas of Black American Innovators.* New York: William Morrow, 1993.
Haber, Louis. *Black Pioneers of Science and Invention.* New York: Harcourt Brace and World, 1970.
Harrison, Paul C. *Black Light: The African-American Hero.* New York: Thunder's Mouth Press, 1993.
Lee, George L. *Interesting People: Black American History Makers.* New York: Ballantine Books, 1989.
Potter, Joan. *African-American Firsts.* Elizabethtown, New York: Pinto Press, 1994.
Stewart, Jeffery C. *1001 Things Everyone Should Know About African-American History.* New York: Doubleday, 1996.

Exercises

Speech Assignments

1. *Demonstration speech.* Deliver a three-to-five-minute speech in which you demonstrate a technique or procedure. Choose something you enjoy doing and do well. Consider whether your audience will see the usefulness of your information. Topics that offer little utility to an audience must be made interesting to hold attention.

Delivery.   This speech should be delivered extemporaneously. Demonstration speeches require freedom of movement. Practice this speech thoroughly so that you can deliver it easily and naturally. The less dependent on your outline or notes you are, the better.

Sample Topics

1. How to remove spots inexpensively
2. How to toss a salad
3. How to wrap a turban
4. How to make a Greek salad
5. How to perform a magic trick

2. *Speech to instruct with visual aid.* Prepare a four-to-six-minute speech to instruct using a visual aid. Choose a subject that you find interesting and whose effectiveness will be increased by the use of a visual aid. Organize your speech carefully, choosing visual aids that will effectively add to the listeners' understanding.

Delivery.   This speech should be delivered extemporaneously. You must be able to move around freely when using an aid. Refer to Chapter 4 for suggestions on how to use visual aids effectively.

Sample Topics

1. The hemispheres of the brain
2. The vampire bat
3. The principle of radar
4. Tax reform
5. The Vikings

3. *Introducing a classmate.* Interview a classmate, questioning her about her hobbies, goals, attitudes, accomplishments, or anything you feel will be of interest to the class. Take careful notes. Then have your classmate interview you. Develop your presentation in an interesting way and put it in an order that will be easy for you and your audience to remember.

Suggestions

1. Pronounce your classmate's name distinctly and correctly.
2. Be as friendly and as enthusiastic as you can.
3. Be accurate. Check your facts before you deliver the speech.
4. Be familiar with your material. If you need notes use only one note card.

11

Persuasion

When you think of the word *persuasion,* what mental picture occurs to you? Do you visualize a TV commercial done by some slick multimillion-dollar advertising agency? Do you picture a political candidate who would promise almost anything if it meant getting elected? Do you envision someone selling condos, used cars, or magazines? Do you see yourself trying to get a few extra days to finish that term paper or pay off that loan? It might very well be that you see all these images and more because in this country persuasion is so much a part of our society and our lives.

We are involved with persuasion daily both as receivers and senders. We are constantly being bombarded with appeals to "get with it," to "enjoy life," and to give ourselves "the very best." We spend a lot of our time talking to others trying to get them to act a certain way, to agree with our point of view, or just simply to like us more.

The two main differences between this one-to-one persuasion and delivering a persuasive speech are that the latter involves talking to more people and spending more time and effort in planning, preparation, and delivery. Otherwise, the methods are basically the same.

Persuasion Defined

Persuasion can be defined as *a conscious attempt to influence the thought or behavior of others through the use of personal, psychological, and logical appeals.* Let us examine this definition in detail.

First, consider the word *conscious.* You must know that your purpose is to persuade. The more aware you are of exactly what you wish to accomplish, the more likely you are to be successful. An informative speech may also persuade, but if its primary purpose is to inform, then the persuasion is accidental.

The second word to remember is *attempt.* Whether you are successful or not, you are still involved in persuasion. The vacuum cleaner salesperson can make a good living delivering the same sales pitch to ten customers a day, even though only two or three of them buy the product.

The third important word is *influence.* You don't have to sell the product immediately to be a successful persuader. Persuasion can be a long-range process, which influences thought or behavior a little at a time. Consider, for example, an attempt to improve the image that minority residents of a major city have of the police department. You can't expect to change overnight attitudes that for some it took years to develop. The best you might be able to expect from some of these citizens is to make them a little less antagonistic toward the police.

Finally, there are three appeals or types of proof in the definition that persuaders use to sell their products more effectively: personal, psychological, and logical.

Personal Proof

Over two thousand years ago the Greek philosopher Aristotle stated that no other factor was more important to success in persuasion than the audience's perception of a persuader as having good sense, good moral character, and goodwill. Speech experts agree that this principle is as true today as it was then. No factor is more important to your success as a persuader than the image your listener has of you as a person. Ideally, you want your audience to see you as a competent person who has integrity and goodwill toward them. If they do, your chances of being successful as a persuader are excellent.

Competence

Competence means being well qualified, having good sense, and knowing what you are talking about. Most of us are influenced by those who are capable. When we have problems with our electronic equipment, we take it to an expert to have it fixed. When our dentist tells us that we need a root canal, we set up an appointment. When our doctor tells us that our appendix must be removed immediately, we agree.

To be an effective persuader you must project an image of competence to your audience. To a great extent this will depend on how much time and effort you put into preparing and delivering your speech. A carefully organized, clearly worded speech is the mark of a competent communicator. Following are five specific suggestions you can use to project an image of competence to your audience:

1. Articulate your words clearly and use correct grammar and pronunciation. A listener is likely to question your ideas if they are unclear or expressed incorrectly.
2. Be up to date. A competent person uses the most current information available.
3. Indicate your qualifications. If you have education or experience that provides you with special knowledge about your subject, indicate this during your introduction.
4. Speak with confidence. One of the characteristics of the competent person is a positive approach.
5. Be fluent. Practice your speech so that you can deliver it easily and naturally. Whether justified or not, listeners often judge nonfluency as an indication of poor preparation or indecision.

Integrity

Have you ever had the feeling that a politician you were listening to was just a little too smooth, or that even though you couldn't put your finger on it, something made you wonder if you could trust a particular salesperson? In today's world, with its hypocrisy and credibility gaps, integrity is of major concern to an audience. Before an audience will accept your ideas they must feel that you are worthy of their trust and respect. Following are specific suggestions that will help you indicate to your audience that you are sincere and honest:

1. Dress appropriately. Your chances of achieving a desired response will be greater if you dress according to the expectations of your audience.
2. Establish a common bond. Listeners are more inclined to respond positively to a speaker they see as having similar attitudes, values, and experiences.
3. Be objective. To be effective, you must show your audience that you are presenting your views fairly and fully.
4. Indicate your motives. If you have strong motives for presenting your viewpoint, indicate these to your audience. Even if they don't agree with you, they will admire your convictions.
5. Be sincere. You are more likely to project an image of sincerity if your tone of voice and facial expression are appropriate to what you are saying.

Goodwill

"The key to success for a salesman is to be well liked," says Willie Loman in Arthur Miller's play *Death of a Salesman*. While this is an oversimplification, being well liked is an important qualification for a salesperson. People are much more apt to buy something from someone they like than from someone they are indifferent to or don't like. Therefore, one of your most important jobs as a persuader is to get your audience to like you. The best way to do this is to show that you like them. Here are some specific suggestions you can use to enhance your image as a person of goodwill:

1. Show enthusiasm. Greeting your audience in a lively, energetic way will show them that you are interested in them and happy to be there.
2. Use tact. You can project an image of good will by being diplomatic and flexible, especially when dealing with an issue to which some of your listeners are opposed.
3. Be respectful. Treat your listeners with courtesy. Give them credit for having ability, uniqueness, and intelligence.
4. Use humor. An attitude of friendliness is projected by a speaker's use of humor. When used effectively, humor causes both the speaker and the audience to relax.
5. Establish rapport. *Rapport* is a French word meaning "to bring harmony." You can establish rapport with your audience by showing that you like them. Whenever you can, make reference to those in your audience. If you are on a first-name basis with some, refer to them whenever it suits the occasion.

Image

In persuasion, the term *image* refers to a mental picture that a customer has of the product that the persuader is selling. That product can be political candidates, a company, a brand of wine, and so on. When you deliver a persuasive speech, the "product" you are selling is you. As you have seen, you want your listeners to have a mental picture of you as a person of competence, integrity, and goodwill. If they do, your personal proof will be strengthened, and the chances that they will believe you will increase.

Credibility

There is a positive relationship between image and credibility: the better the image, the better the credibility. Conversely, a person with a poor image has low credibility. The strength of personal proof can clearly be demonstrated by examining the image-credibility relationship of Dr. Martin Luther King, Jr. As a highly educated, renowned speaker and writer, this national figure projected an image of competence. As a Baptist minister, civil rights leader, and winner of the Nobel Peace Prize, he projected an image of integrity. And as a leader who was so close to his followers that he marched with them, slept with them, and went to jail with them, he projected an image of good will. Among his supporters King's credibility was so high that many of them risked harassment, jail, personal injury, and even their lives to follow him.

Psychological Proof

The second appeal used by persuaders to sell their products is psychological proof. Psychological proof appeals to the attitudes and motives of the audience. We tend to act in certain ways because of two factors: attitude and motive. Attitude often determines the way we are going to act, and motive supplies the impulse or desire to act.

Attitudes

Attitudes are learned. We form them from our education and experience and from our interaction with others. For example, we form favorable or unfavorable attitudes about government, religion, abortion, communism, sex, and so on. These attitudes give direction to our behavior causing us to act in predisposed ways in different situations.

Motives

The inner drive or impulse that stimulates behavior is called *motive*. If you consider attitude as the directive force of behavior, motive could be considered the driving force. There are two basic types of motives: physical motives and social motives.

Physical Motives

Often referred to as basic human drives, physical motives are common to people of all societies. All of us are born with the same basic physiological needs. We want to eat when hungry, drink when thirsty, defend ourselves when threatened, seek safety from the weather, and so on. For many of us in the United States, these basic needs are being abundantly satisfied. And the more money we have, the more we spend to achieve the greatest possible comfort. We buy central air conditioning, contour furniture, and heated swimming pools to pamper our most priceless possession, ourselves. We are, to a great extent, creatures of the body. Although it is unlikely that you will encounter a situation where your listeners have not satisfied their physical needs, making them aware of those who have not can often be quite effective.

Social Motives

A baby is born with a set of physical motives but without social motives. These are learned. No doubt the first social motive the infant develops is the security motive. This motive is primary to the newborn baby and continues as a powerful need at least until the child goes off to school. The tendency of little children to cuddle up; carry a doll, teddy bear, or security blanket around; or hide behind mother when a stranger comes to the door are all examples of the strength of this motive in the small child.

Another motive that develops during this period of closeness to the mother is the approval motion. The baby soon learns that cooing, smiling, laughing, and the like, win approval. The child also soon finds that while some things win a pat on the back, others result in a pat on the backside. Approval becomes an important need for the child. For some children the need for approval is so strong that isolation becomes a significant punishment. Banishing a child to his or her room with the comment, "Go to your room. I don't want to see you any more today," can be devastating for some. During this time, children also develop their own attitudes of approval or disapproval toward themselves.

Specific Motive Appeals

Sex

Perhaps no motive is appealed to more often in persuasion than the sex motive. Advertising in this country is supersaturated with sex to sell everything from shock absorbers to perfume. CDs are sold with covers featuring attractive women or handsome men who have absolutely no relationship to the music inside. Automobiles, cigarettes, toothpaste, and diet sodas are all used by young, vibrant, "beautiful" people, and if you use these products, somehow you will be beautiful too. Be assured, the sex motive plays an important role in all areas of persuasion.

Security

Another appeal often used in advertising is the security motive. The effect that this motive has on us and our loved ones is clearly evident in today's society. We have banks to protect our money, unions to protect our jobs, and insurance companies to provide for our health care, and when the time comes, for our survivors.

We go to college to provide for a more secure future, we "go steady" to ensure a dependable date, and we put money aside for a "rainy day." In this age of violence and uncertainty, no generation has been as security minded as this one.

Approval

Whether it be at home, at work, at school, or among friends, we are constantly seeking the approval of others. Any advertisement that features brand names is selling approval along with the product. A person might spend months landscaping a backyard or painting a picture for the satisfaction of being able to say, "I made this myself."

One effective technique in persuasion is to take the feeling of approval away from an individual, making the person feel uncomfortable. An example is the priest, rabbi, or minister making hell "hot" for the congregation. Another example is the ad that talks about the starving children of the world, pointing out that the average dog in this country eats better than many children in the rest of the world or that the average American citizen throws away enough garbage per day to feed a family of six in India. The idea is that the readers or listeners feel uncomfortable about the situation until they contribute their money in an effort to help.

Conformity

Closely related to the approval motive is the motive to conform. Even in the most primitive societies, people have customs, mores, and rules to which they must conform in order to live in harmony with their peers. Most people tend to go along with the group rather than swim against the stream. Have you ever, for example, worn a style that was not particularly becoming to you because it was the thing to do? Or would you dare show up in jeans at a formal dance?

Early in life you learned to conform to the expectations of those around you. As you grew older and came in contact with more people, you found that conforming to these expectations became considerably more difficult. You could, for example, be labeled un-American for conforming to the expectations of a Christian "peace group" or un-Christian for advocating the nuclear destruction of Communist nations.

Success

The desire to succeed can be a powerful motive. For some it is so intense that it overshadows all others. Individuals have been so strongly motivated to succeed that they have lied, cheated, and even killed to further this ambition. Advertisers have used the success motive to sell products ranging from toothpaste to condominiums. The success motive has long been used to sell luxury cars. People who buy Mercedes, Cadillacs, Porsches, and Lexus are buying success along with the automobile.

Creativity

Creativity is one of the motives that can be unusually forceful. It is a form of self-actualization. Some have spent years of self-sacrifice and deprivation in an attempt to develop an artistic or musical ability. Who hasn't heard of a starving artist's sale or an author who could paper a room with rejection slips from publishers. The fact that these people continue creating testifies to the strength of this motive.

It should be pointed out that while a person may be more influenced by one motive than another at any given time, motives seldom operate individually. Sometimes two or more motives combine to affect a person's behavior. A person might be motivated to lift weights for a number of reasons. Weight lifting conditions the body, satisfying the good health motive. It develops muscles and a trim figure, satisfying both approval and popularity motives.

At other times motives are in conflict with each other. Take, for example, the person who attends a party where drugs are being used. To refuse to go along with the group can threaten that person's popularity and peer approval, but to use the drugs can be a threat to security and parental approval. As you can see, motives have a significant impact on people's lives.

Logical Proof

Reasoning is the process of drawing conclusions from evidence. There are two kinds of evidence: evidence of fact and evidence of opinion. The explanation of this reasoning process to others in an attempt to influence belief is called "argumentation." A basic argument consists of two statements: a premise and a conclusion drawn from that premise. Here are two basic arguments:

1. Mark is a member of the American Nazi party. Therefore, he is a troublemaker.
2. Mark has been arrested three times. Therefore, he is a troublemaker.

Both statements involve a premise–conclusion relationship. In the first example the conclusion is drawn from the fact that Mark is a member of the American Nazi party. "Mark is a member of the American Nazi party. Therefore, he is a troublemaker." This argument is based on deductive reasoning. You have come to the conclusion that Mark is a troublemaker because he belongs to the American Nazi party. You reason from a general premise (members of the American Nazi party are troublemakers) to a minor premise (Mark is a member of the American Nazi party) to the conclusion (therefore, Mark is a troublemaker). Whenever you reason from a general rule to a specific case, you are reasoning deductively.

The second statement, "Mark has been arrested three times. Therefore, he is a troublemaker," is an example of inductive reasoning. There is no rule to guide the reasoner, only the observation about Mark: He has been arrested three times. Therefore, he is a troublemaker. When you come to a conclusion as the result of observing or experiencing individual situations or cases, you are using inductive reasoning. Although you may not have been aware of it, you have used this form of reasoning throughout your life. Do you like pizza? Enjoy rock music? Think that you are a good student? Whether your answer to these questions is yes or no, it has undoubtedly been based on inductive reasoning. You probably decided whether you liked pizza after eating one, three, five, or more. The same was true about your attitude toward rock music and your status as a student. Your observation or experience with these involvements has determined your conclusion.

Deductive Reasoning

As you can see, induction draws conclusions from specific experiences or observations, and deduction begins with the acceptance of a general rule (as stated in a major premise) and applies it to a specific case in the conclusion. In most cases deductive reasoning is stated in a form called an "enthymeme," where one of the premises or sometimes the conclusion is not expressed but implied. This was the case with the deductive statement above: Mark is a member of the American Nazi party. Therefore, he is a troublemaker.

When formally stated, deduction is expressed in a three-step pattern called a "syllogism." The reasoning moves from a major premise to a minor premise to a conclusion. In the example above the major premise was not expressed but implied. The formally stated syllogism would appear this way:

Major premise: Members of the American Nazi party are troublemakers.
Minor premise: Mark is a member of the American Nazi party.
Conclusion: Therefore, Mark is a troublemaker.

It is often useful to examine a syllogism by putting it in this formal, three-step form. This makes it easier to determine: (1) whether the major and minor premises are true, and (2) whether the conclusion follows logically from them. A syllogism is like a framework for deductive logic.

Keep in mind that while inductive reasoning moves from specific instances to a general conclusion, deductive moves from a general rule (heavy smokers are likely to get lung cancer) to a minor premise (Helga is a heavy smoker) to a specific conclusion (therefore, Helga is likely to get lung cancer).

In order to use deductive reasoning effectively as a speaker, you must get your audience to agree with your major and minor premises and present a conclusion that follows logically from the premises. To do this, you will need to support your premises with evidence.

Suppose, for instance, that you are delivering a speech on the undesirability of eating too many meals at fast-food restaurants, and one of your points is that much of the food served in fast-food restaurants is extremely high in cholesterol. Your deductive argument would be expressed in a syllogism similar to this one:

Major premise: High-cholesterol foods are dangerous to your health.

Minor premise: The food served at fast-food restaurants is mostly high in cholesterol.

Conclusion: Therefore, the food served at fast-food restaurants is dangerous to your health.

Now that you have constructed the syllogism, you need to get your audience to agree with your premises. If they accept your premises as true, and if the premises are set up properly, then they will agree with your conclusion if it follows logically from the premises. First you will have to present evidence to get your audience to agree with your major premise: High-cholesterol foods are dangerous to your health. You might quote the testimony of one or two experts on the subject. Choose people your audience will consider objective and well qualified. You could quote recent statistics or research studies. Perhaps an explanation of the effects of cholesterol on the body would be effective.

When you have supported your major premise adequately, you are ready to deal with the minor premise: The food served at fast-food restaurants is mostly high in cholesterol. Certainly, you would give examples of the kinds of high-cholesterol foods you are talking about: hamburgers, french fries, fish fried in animal fat, and the like. Following this you might use comparative statistics to show the contrast between these foods and the kinds you would eat in a well-balanced diet.

If you have succeeded in getting your listeners to agree with your premises, they will accept your conclusion: Therefore, the food served in fast-food restaurants is dangerous to your health. The test of a good conclusion must always be, Does it follow logically from the evidence that has been presented? If you have supplied your listeners with enough evidence to get them to accept your major and minor premises, they will accept your conclusion. When used correctly, deductive reasoning can be an effective form of persuasion.

Inductive Reasoning

As you have seen, deductive reasoning moves essentially from a general rule to a specific conclusion. Inductive reasoning, on the other hand, reverses this process. When you reason inductively, you examine specific instances and as a result of your observations come to a general conclusion. For example, if you have had good service from three cars, a Pontiac, a Chevrolet, and a Buick, you might come to the conclusion that a General Motors product is a good car to own. If you have read statistics that show people with college degrees earn far more than those who are less educated, then you might have concluded that college is the place for you. Both of these forms of reasoning are primarily inductive. The first, generalization, examines individual cases—three GM automobiles—and concludes that what is true about these specific cars is also true about GM products in general. The second, statistics, involves drawing conclusions from numerical evidence. If the figures show that people with college degrees earn more, then the chances are that if you get a higher education, you will make more money too. Let us look at these two forms of inductive reasoning in more detail.

Reasoning by Generalization

This type of reasoning involves examining specific details or examples and coming to a general conclusion. If there are a limited number of instances involved, the more you cite, the more probable the conclusions. For example, you might argue that Senator Jones is prolabor and Senator Smith antilabor by citing their voting records on legislation affecting labor.

When used well, generalization can be an effective argument in persuasion. Carefully controlled scientific experiments and studies can provide strong evidence for your speeches.

Reasoning by Statistics

This form of inductive argument involves drawing conclusions from numerical evidence. Many people are suspicious of statistics. It has been said that one can prove anything with numbers. However, when used properly, statistics can provide a compelling argument. One example of statistics that works is the poll predicting the winner in an upcoming election. By taking a random sampling from a cross section of the voting population in a given area, pollsters can accurately predict the outcome of that election. Another example is the controlled test. Ten thousand people are tested to determine the effectiveness of a new vaccine. If the vaccine is effective for 98 percent of the test group, it will probably be effective for 98 percent of the total population. When used properly, statistics can be very persuasive. Here are a number of suggestions to follow when using statistics:

1. *Document statistics.* When the statistics you are using are consistent with the general knowledge and experience of your audience, there is no need to indicate their exact source. However, when using statistics that are not widely known, indicate when and by whom the statistics were compiled.
2. *Make statistics clear.* Since it is quite likely that some in your audience have been deceived in the past by statistics, it is important that you explain statistics clearly whenever you use them.
3. *Round off statistics.* When dealing with large numbers, it is a good idea to round them off. Instead of saying that the population of Denmark is 5,163,000, round it off to an approximate five million.
4. *Dramatize statistics.* If you can dramatize your statistics, they are more likely to be understood and remembered. For example, to say, "In Hong Kong, one person in fifty is an opium user, and a habit there costs about $650 a year to support," dramatizes the problem much more effectively than giving a statistical percentage.

Other Forms of Reasoning

Reasoning by generalization and by statistics is primarily inductive. However, reasoning by comparison and by cause and effect mixes induction and deduction.

Reasoning by Comparison

Argument by comparison involves the examination of two similar cases. If the two have enough similarities, it is possible to argue that what is true of one case will be true of the others as well. The comparisons may be either literal or figurative. Literal comparisons compare things that are within the same categories, such as U.S. inflation rates in 1987 and 1988 and a comparison of academic standards at different universities. If the similarities in the literal comparisons are significant, the conclusions often appear logical.

Figurative comparisons point out similarities between things in different categories. Comparisons between life and a pathway and between the kingdom of heaven and a sower of seeds are examples of figurative comparisons. Although figurative comparisons are often weak as arguments since they are based on only one major similarity, they are both popular and colorful and also useful in relating the unknown to the known.

Reasoning from Cause and Effect

Causal reasoning is based on the principle that every cause has an effect. When two things occur together with any frequency, we might naturally determine that one is caused by the other. For example, the person who complains, "Every time I eat pizza, I get heartburn," might logically assume that the pizza has triggered the heartburn. However, since cause-and-effect relationships can often be quite complicated, it could be that the heartburn is caused by a gallbladder disorder, which is aggravated by eating the pizza, so that rather than giving up pizza, the person should see a doctor.

Causal relationships are most clearly demonstrated in carefully controlled situations. For example, a number of years ago researchers were interested in finding out what effect music had on the milk production of dairy cows. They used two experimental groups and a control group. Each group of cows was housed in the same size barn, fed the same food, and matched in every relevant way, except that after the first week, light classical music was piped into barn A, hard rock into barn B, and no music into barn C. The results of the experiment, which ended after week 2, were that group A produced half again as much milk as they had during week 1, group B's production was reduced by one-third, and group C's production remained the same. The experiment showed clearly what effect the music had on the cows.

Keep in mind that causal relationships are more difficult to identify in less controlled situations. This is especially true in political, economic, and social situations, which frequently have multiple causes.

Fallacies

Fallacious reasoning can be the result of faulty induction or deduction, or the acceptance of misleading argumentation. Some of these fallacies occur so often that they have been isolated and labeled. The most common of these are treated below.*

Unwarranted or Hasty Generalization

A generalization is fallacious when it is based on insufficient or unfair evidence, or when it is not warranted by the facts available. For example, "All hippies are dirty," "All welfare recipients are lazy," and so on.

Errors in Causal Induction

Fallacy in causal induction occurs when there is no logical relationship between a cause and an effect. Two most common cause-and-effect fallacies are *post hoc* (after this, therefore, because of this) and *non sequitur* (it does not follow).

Post Hoc
Post hoc is the fallacy of thinking that an event which follows another is necessarily caused by the other. Thus, you might conclude that the Democratic party promotes war, that television viewing increases juvenile delinquency, and that an easing of censorship causes an increase in immorality.

The error in post hoc reasoning occurs because the reasoner ignores other factors which may have contributed to the effect. A survey of former college debaters revealed, for example, that they were considerably more successful in their chosen field of work than their nondebating counterparts. To assume from this that their experience as debaters was the cause of their success would be fallacious. Other factors must be considered: Students who become debaters usually possess superior verbal ability, have keen analytical minds, and are highly motivated by competition. No doubt these factors, which led them into debate, also contributed to their success.

*This section is taken with permission from Arthur Koch and Stanley B. Felber, *What Did You Say?* 3rd ed. (Englewood Cliffs, NJ: Prentice-Hall, 1985).

Non Sequitur
In this fallacy the conclusion reached does not necessarily follow from the facts argued. The argument that because a man is kind to animals he will make a good husband ignores the possibilities that the man may make a bad husband, drink excessively, cheat, or beat his wife.

Begging the Question

An argument begs the question when it assumes something as true when it actually needs to be proven. For instance, the declaration that "these corrupt laws must be changed" asserts the corruption but does not prove it, and consequently the conclusion is not justified.

Begging the question also occurs when we make a charge and then insist that someone else disprove it. For example, to answer the question, "How do you know that the administration is honest?" would put the respondent in the position of trying to disprove a conclusion which was never proven in the first place. Remember, whoever makes an assertion has the burden of proof.

Ignoring the Question

Ignoring the question occurs when the argument shifts from the original subject to a different one, or when the argument appeals to some emotional attitude which has nothing to do with the logic of the case. An example of the first would be a man replying, "Haven't you ever done anything dishonest?" when accused of cheating on his wife. He ignores the question of his infidelity by shifting to a different argument.

An argument that appeals to the emotional attitudes of the reader or listener would be the statement, "No good American would approve of this communistic proposal."

False Analogy

To argue by analogy is to compare two things which are alike in germane known respects and to suggest that they will also be alike in unknown respects. This method is accurate if the things being compared are genuinely similar: "George will do well in graduate school; he had an excellent academic record as an undergraduate." It is likely to be fallacious when they are dissimilar: "There's nothing to handling a snowmobile; it's just like riding a bicycle."

Analogies are more difficult to prove when the comparison is figurative rather than literal. In a political campaign, the incumbent might admonish the voter "not to change horses in the middle of the stream," while the opponent replies that "a new broom sweeps clean."

Either/or Fallacy

The either/or fallacy is reasoning that concludes there are only two choices to an argument when there are other possible alternatives. A tragic example would be the reasoning that escalated the Vietnam War. The argument was: Either we fight and win in Vietnam or all of Southeast Asia will fall to the Communists. Of course, we didn't win and all of Southeast Asia didn't fall to the Communists.

Ad Hominem

In this fallacy the argument shifts from the proposition to the character of the opponent. Unfortunately, this abuse often occurs in politics, and the voters who fall for it wind up casting their votes against a candidate rather than for one. "I wouldn't trust him. He cheated on his wife," or "You're not going to believe a former convict?" are examples of this fallacy.

Red Herring

The red herring is similar to the ad hominem fallacy but does not attack the opponent's character. It gets its name from the superstition that if you drag a red herring across your path it will throw any wild animals following you off the track. Information is introduced that is not relevant to the question at hand in the hope that it will divert attention from the real issue. In politics an opposing candidate is pictured as being overly religious, ultrarich, or divorced. If the trait has nothing to do with the way he will perform in office, the argument is a red herring.

Ad Populum

The *ad populum* argument appeals to the theory that whatever the masses believe is true. Make no mistake; popularity is not always an accurate determiner of truth. Consider the landslide victory of Richard Nixon in 1972. A typical ad populum fallacy is: "Unconditional amnesty is wrong, because most people are against it."

Types of Persuasive Speeches

Persuasive speeches can be classified into three types: (1) speeches to convince; (2) speeches to reinforce; and (3) speeches to actuate. Careful audience analysis is essential in persuasive speaking. The type of persuasion a speaker chooses should be based upon the attitudes of the audience prior to the speech and the specific changes sought.

Speeches to Convince

At times a persuader must deal with an audience that is either undecided, indifferent, or opposed to a proposition.

President Clinton defending his health plan, Jesse Jackson arguing against invading Haiti, a college debater attempting to prove that capital punishment is desirable, and a student senate leader trying to convince fellow students that the student senate is doing a good job are all cases of persuasion to convince.

Because speeches to convince appeal to the listener's intelligence rather than emotions, they employ logical rather than psychological or personal appeals. They must rely on clear reasoning and carefully selected evidence in order to get listeners to respond satisfactorily. Six forms of supporting evidence: examples, explanation, statistics, testimony, comparison/contrast, and visual aids were presented in detail in Chapter 4 under supporting devices. A review of Chapter 4 should help you develop the speech to convince.

Speeches to Reinforce

Rather than appealing to their intelligence, a speech to reinforce appeals essentially to the motives, attitudes, and sentiments of an audience. Rather than being undecided, indifferent, or opposed, the audience is in agreement with the speaker's point of view.

On Veterans Day a speaker reminds the audience of the sacrifices made by those who fought and died so that each of them might enjoy this land of freedom. Those in the audience already believe that the sacrifices made by these veterans were important. However, the speaker wants to strengthen that belief, to reinforce that appreciation, to deepen that concern.

The Independence Day orator, the speaker at a pep rally, the commencement speaker, the preacher, and the persons delivering eulogies, inaugural addresses, memorials, and testimonials are involved with persuasion to reinforce. Their purpose is to strengthen the existing attitudes, sentiments, emotions, and beliefs of their audience.

Speeches to Actuate

The speech to actuate calls for a specific action on the part of the audience. It asks them to buy, to join, to march, to sign. A speech to convince may attempt to create an awareness in the audience as to the danger to our society caused by easy access to handguns; the speech to actuate seeks to get those in the audience to write to their representatives in Congress urging them to vote to get handguns off the streets. A speech to reinforce may seek to arouse greater concern for the plight of the hungry in our society; the speech to actuate would seek an overt response asking the audience for a specific donation of food or money to respond directly to the problem.

While the speech to actuate may employ the logical and psychological appeals used in speeches to convince and reinforce, the purpose of this speech is to get specific action. For this reason, speeches to actuate are generally more successful when directed at audiences that basically agree with the persuader's point of view.

Sample Speech and Commentary

Below is the text and commentary of a persuasive speech delivered by a student in a public speaking class at the Milwaukee Area Technical College. It provides a clear model of a speech to actuate.

Sample Speech to Actuate

Do Yourself a Favor: Jog.*   (See commentary on page 150.)

1. *Introduction.* Have you ever had a problem that you tried hard to solve but couldn't? Sure you have and so have I. When I first came to this school, I was out of shape physically, about twenty pounds overweight, and emotionally depressed. Now, six months later, I realize that all three of my problems had the same cause: I wasn't exercising enough. It wasn't that I hadn't tried. I had tried racquetball, softball, volleyball, and tennis. I didn't stay with any of them. Part of the problem was that with each of these activities, I had to set aside regular hours, but my schedule changed from day to day. Then one day, I picked up a copy of Jim Fixx's book on running, and I began considering jogging as an exercise. I read a few more books on jogging and found out some interesting facts. First, no matter what your age, if you are in good physical condition, you can jog. A child can begin jogging when he or she is old enough to run safely. An adult in good physical condition can jog at virtually any age. I read about one seventy-eight-year-old man who recently completed the grueling twenty-six mile San Francisco Marathon. I figured that if someone that old could jog, so could I. Another advantage for me was that a person can jog any time, day or night. It sounded like a plan, so I began to jog. I have been jogging now for about six months, and I feel better physically and mentally, and my friends tell me that I look better too. What it all comes down to is this:

Thesis statement: Jogging is the ideal exercise.

---

*Source: Used with permission of the speaker, Kai Koch.

Preview Statement: This talk will examine three benefits of jogging. First, that it strengthens the heart; Second, that it aids in removing unwanted fat; and Third, that it develops good emotional balance.

(Transition: The first benefit I mentioned is that jogging strengthens the heart.)

2. *Body.* The advantage of a strong heart is that it pumps blood more efficiently, working less and resting more. As you can see from this chart, jogging strengthens the heart in four ways: (1) it improves collateral (auxiliary) circulation; (2) it increases the efficiency of the heart in extracting oxygen from the blood; (3) it lowers the fat concentration in the blood; and (4) it lowers blood pressure. These benefits to the heart significantly reduce the risk of heart attack and stroke. A scientific study of the benefits of jogging administered to a group of Harvard graduates indicated that the rate of heart attacks for those who exercised the equivalent of twenty miles of jogging per week was 39 percent below those who exercised lightly or not at all.

Notice on the chart that when some arteries become narrowed by fatty deposits those nearby open up new branches to maintain an adequate blood supply. This is called collateral circulation. Jogging also reduces the fatty deposits along with improving the efficiency of the heart in extracting oxygen from the blood. Since you pump seventy two thousand quarts of blood through your body every twenty four hours these factors also lower your blood pressure.

(Transition: You've seen that jogging strengthens the heart in four ways but how does it reduce fat?)

Second, jogging aids in removing unwanted fat. Whatever extra weight the runner is carrying makes running more difficult. Therefore, the incentive to lose weight increases. Losing weight often improves a person's physical appearance, but, more importantly, it can significantly improve one's health. Dr. Kenneth Cooper, a renowned authority on aerobics, states: " . . . obesity may be a more mysterious killer than many people expect." He estimates that more than fifty million Americans are seriously obese, collectively carrying more than one billion pounds of extra weight. Anyone who is more than 15 percent heavier than his or her ideal weight is considered obese. Getting rid of that extra weight could add years to a person's life, and jogging can help you to accomplish this objective. A recent survey that appeared in *Runners' World* magazine showed that two-thirds of the runners who responded had lost between ten and twenty pounds through jogging.

This next chart indicates the number of calories a person of a particular weight will expend while running between five to eight miles per hour. If you set up a routine of running five to eight miles per day you will find that without even dieting you will lose unwanted fat and make your running even easier.

(Transition: So far you've heard what jogging can do for your body. Now I'm going to tell you what it can do for your emotional well-being.)

Third, jogging develops good emotional balance. Perhaps the most important prerequisite of emotional well-being is a good self-concept. In her book *The Psychic Power of Running,* Valerie Andrews calls jogging "the ultimate exercise and man's healthiest activity." She says that jogging combines the achievement of physical fitness with the satisfaction of self-actualization. A jogger almost always experiences a boost in self-confidence due to his or her improved physical condition. This is often accomplished by a feeling of fulfillment and self-worth. The emotional benefits of jogging are well-documented. A controlled experiment at the University of Wisconsin by Dr. John Greist found jogging far superior to psychotherapy as a treatment for patients with clinical depression. This coincides with a view widely accepted among psychologists and psychiatrists who see this exercise resulting in lowered levels of depression and anxiety.

(Pre-summary transition. Well, today I've shared with you how I got into jogging and what it has done for me. I have discussed how jogging strengthens the heart, aids in removing unwanted fat, and provides emotional balance. I'm sold on jogging but you have to make up your own mind.)

3. *Conclusion.* As you have heard, the benefits of jogging are impressive. The fact that it strengthens the heart, lessening the risk of heart attack, stroke, and heart disease could prolong your life. The emotional balance it provides will help to reduce your anxiety and increase your ability to handle stress. Finally, the fact that it aids in reducing unwanted fat will improve both your health and appearance. These are all good reasons for starting this ideal exercise. So, pick up a book on jogging and follow the instructions, get approval from your physician if you are in doubt about your physical condition, and start jogging.

Bibliography
Andrews, Valerie. *The Psychic Power of Running.* New York: Ballantine Books, 1979.

Cooper, Kenneth. *The Aerobics Program for Total Well-Being.* New York: M. Evans, 1982.

"Dietary Habits of Runners," in *The Complete Runner,* eds. of Runners World Magazine. New York: Avon, 1978.

Fixx, Jim. *Jim Fixx's Second Book of Running.* New York: Random House, 1980.

Mirkin, Gabe, and Marshall Hoffman. *The Sportsmedicine Book.* Boston: Little, Brown, 1978.

Morgan, William P. "The Mind of a Marathoner," *Psychology Today,* April 1978, pp. 43–46.

Commentary

In the introduction, the speaker gains attention with a rhetorical question and introduces the deductive premise that people who are out of shape, over-weight, and depressed have problems. He gains credibility by establishing a common bond with his listeners as a fellow student and indicating to them that he has read a number of books on jogging. He then introduces three premises: (1) jogging strengthens the heart, (2) it aids in removing unwanted fat, and (3) it develops good emotional balance. These premises lead to the conclusion and central idea that jogging is the ideal exercise for them. Listing these premises also previews the main points to be covered in the speech. Finally, the speaker indicates that the purpose of the speech is to persuade the audience to try jogging as an exercise.

In the first body paragraph, the speaker uses explanation, visual aids, testimony, statistics, and comparison to support the premise that jogging strengthens the heart. The speaker appeals to the listener's motive of security in pointing out that the risk of heart attack is much less for those who jog twenty miles or more per week.

In the second body paragraph, the speaker appeals to the listener's motives of approval, popularity, and security. Losing weight will make you look better and avoid the danger of the "mysterious killer," obesity. He uses explanation, testimony, example, and statistics to support the premise that jogging aids in removing unwanted fat.

In the third body paragraph, the speaker appeals to the listener's motives of approval, success, and security by pointing out that jogging improves self-concept and promotes self-actualization by making a person more physically fit and less anxious or depressed. He uses testimony, explanation, statistics, and comparison to support the premise that jogging develops good emotional balance.

In the conclusion, the speaker uses the techniques of summary and restate-ment to remind the audience of the main points of the speech and its central idea. He then ends with a call for action from the audience.

Exercises

1. *Persuasion to reinforce.* Develop a three-to-four-minute speech to reinforce. Remember, persuasion to reinforce is directed at an audience that already agrees with you. You are seeking to make that agreement stronger. Rely chiefly on psychological proof. Appeal to your audience's motives, attitudes, and sentiments.

Delivery.   The speech to reinforce seeks to strengthen the audience's beliefs. It is imperative that they feel the speaker is sincere. The more relaxed and spontaneous you are, the more likely it will be that you will succeed.

Sample Central Ideas

1. We are all unique.
2. You can make a difference.
3. We owe senior citizens a lot.
4. Be proud of our flag.

2. *Persuasion to convince.* Develop a three-to-four-minute speech supporting a point of view you feel many in your audience are either undecided about or are against. Appeal to your audience's intelligence. Present your material objectively and fairly. An audience will react negatively to a speaker they perceive as being biased.

Suggestions

1. Try to establish a common bond with your audience.
2. Try to show your listeners that your motives are sincere.
3. Don't attempt too much in this assignment. If you can get those in your audience to modify their views even slightly, you will have been effective.

Sample Central Ideas

1. The United States should adopt a system of socialized medicine.
2. The U.S. government should prohibit the sale of handguns.
3. The death penalty should be reestablished (abolished) in our state.
4. Our military budget should be reduced by one-third.

3. *Persuasion to actuate.* Develop a two-to-three-minute speech to persuade your audience to act in a particular way. Make clear to your audience exactly what you want them to do. Remember, you are asking your audience to act: to sign, to vote, to buy, to march, to donate, or to participate. Be realistic. Don't ask them to do something they are unlikely to do.

Sample Central Ideas

1. Begin an exercise program.
2. Do a fire check of your home.
3. Hug a loved one today.
4. Avoid using loaded words.

12

Group Communication

If you are like most people, you participate in some form of group discussion almost daily. There are all kinds of group discussions. They may be planned or spontaneous, structured or unstructured, formal or informal, permanent or temporary. Some discussions take place with a group of friends over coffee or with fellow workers during the lunch hour. Others occur in the home where everything from the high cost of living to what to do about the neighbor's dog may be covered. More and more, however, discussions are occurring more formally in organized committees and action groups.

During the last decade citizens have become increasingly involved in the affairs of their communities. Organizations like MADD (Mothers Against Drunk Driving) and CUB (Citizens' Utility Board) have sprung up as a result of people demanding to have a voice in determining policies that affect their lives.

Discussions are also a vital part of formal education. Many instructors employ a lecture–discussion format, and group discussion is often used in classes to promote learning. The advantages of becoming a more effective participant in discussion are obvious. A study of the principles of group discussion, together with guided practice, will help you achieve this goal.

The Functions of Discussion

In general, discussion has four functions: social, educative, therapeutic, and problem solving.

Social Discussion

Social discussion usually occurs spontaneously and is temporary, unstructured, and informal. A typical example of social discussion would be a group of students sitting around a table in the student union discussing federal budget cuts in aid-to-education programs. Another example might be a group of businessmen discussing federal budget cuts from an entirely different viewpoint over cocktails at the nineteenth hole of the local country club. Neither group will resolve the problem they are discussing. However, many of the participants will benefit from the interchange of ideas, the reinforcement of attitudes, and the enjoyment that social discussion groups provide.

Educative Discussion

The function of educative discussion (sometimes called information-seeking discussion) is to make you better informed about the topic discussed. Examples of educative discussion groups include garden clubs, Bible study groups, musical societies, and book clubs. One of the most familiar examples of educative discussion is classroom discussion, which is particularly well suited to the speech class. A brief discussion following each classroom speech can provide valuable feedback to both the speaker and the audience. An all-class discussion of the textbook and the exams will help students better understand speech principles and what is expected of them in the class.

Therapeutic Discussion

A third function of discussion is the therapeutic group. The leader of this group is almost always a trained therapist, whose goal is the personal improvement of each member. Examples of therapeutic groups include alcohol and drug rehabilitation groups, marriage counseling groups, religious encounter groups, and weight-watching groups. These provide a supportive atmosphere where individuals can learn why they act the way they do and what they can do to change their behavior.

Problem-Solving Discussion

Group problem solving is superior to individual problem solving for a number of reasons. First, an individual's background and experience can seldom match those of a group. The more people working on a problem, the more information available to solve it. Second, the more people you have looking at a problem, the more likely you are to solve it correctly. In a group an error by one individual is likely to be spotted by someone else.

As our society grows increasingly complex, more and more problems that must be dealt with are surfacing. The majority of them will be addressed in problem-solving group discussion. In governmental committee meetings, business conferences, church councils, legislative sessions, classroom meetings, and the like, problems are being solved, policies are being determined, and decisions are being made that affect the lives of millions of people. As an educated person, you will be called on to participate in a variety of discussion situations. A study of the principles of group communication, together with guided practice, will help you to develop the knowledge and skill necessary for effective participation.

Types of Discussion

Since the discussion groups you participate in will most likely be either educative or problem solving, the rest of this chapter will concentrate only on these. The six basic types of discussion are the roundtable, the panel, the symposium, the lecture forum, the dialogue, and the interview.

The Roundtable

In the roundtable discussion the participants sit at a round table or in a circle. There are two reasons for this seating arrangement: (1) when seated in a circle, everyone is in a position to maintain eye contact with the others while speaking or listening to them, and (2) no one is seated in a superior "head of the table" position. Each participant is in a position equal to that of his or her neighbor. Everyone, including the moderator or leader if there is one, is involved in a roundtable discussion. There is no audience. This type of discussion is particularly suited to council and committee meetings, conferences, and classroom discussions. Although roundtable discussions usually involve from three to fifteen members, an effective classroom discussion can be held with as many as twenty-five.

The Panel

A panel usually consists of from three to six panelists and a moderator. The members sit in front of an audience or judge in a circle or semicircle so that they can see and react to each other. The language used by panel members is usually informal and conversational. Although panel participants are often made aware of the discussion problem beforehand, most panels are unrehearsed to ensure spontaneity and enthusiasm during the presentation.

Panels that are followed by an audience participation period, or forum, are usually timed. For example, for a one-hour program, forty minutes might be set aside for the panel and twenty minutes for the forum period. It is the moderator's job to summarize the discussion and field the questions from the audience.

The Symposium

Unlike roundtable and panel discussions, which are like magnified conversations, the symposium consists of a series of prepared speeches, each dealing with a specific aspect of the same topic. The number of speakers for a symposium usually ranges from three to five. A time limit is given to each of the speakers, who talk directly to the audience rather than to each other. The moderator opens the discussion, introduces each speaker and topic, and summarizes the discussion at the conclusion. If there is a forum period following the summary, the moderator fields the questions, rephrasing them when necessary.

The Lecture Forum

The lecture forum involves a moderator and a lecturer, who delivers a prepared speech on a subject. The speech is followed by a forum period. The job of the moderator is to introduce the subject and speaker and preside during the forum period. The lecture forum technique has long been used by classroom teachers and political candidates, who then field questions from the audience.

Another variation of the lecture forum is the film forum. The success of this technique is largely dependent on the quality of the film shown and the ability of the moderator to deal effectively with any questions the audience may have regarding the film.

The Dialogue

A dialogue is an interchange and discussion of ideas between two people. It is highly successful when both participants know their subjects well. The dialogue can be a useful classroom exercise. It is an excellent means of communicating information. For best results, the dialogue should be carefully planned so that both participants know where the discussion is heading.

The Interview

A carefully planned interview can be an excellent way to communicate information. In the discussion interview, the participants should plan the questions in advance so both will know where the discussion is going. A good interviewer can elicit a wealth of information from a well-informed interviewee.

In the job interview, found at the end of this chapter, both the interviewer and interviewee should plan their questions separately.

Role-Playing

An excellent way to introduce a discussion problem is through the technique of role-playing. In role-playing the players take part in a brief drama built on a "real-life" problem. The actors in the drama each take the part of a specific character in the problem. They then act out the situation, expressing the views they feel the character they are playing would have. The drama is unrehearsed, and the problem is usually given to the participants on the day the role-playing is to take place.

Role-playing can be an effective way of pretesting a situation. Skill in handling oneself in an interview could make the difference between a student's getting a job or missing it. A series of mock interviews with students playing the roles of personnel director and interviewee provides excellent practice. Students will derive a greater feeling of confidence toward the interview situation and an increased understanding of management's position as well.

Role-playing is particularly useful in clarifying a situation. Often, after seeing the roles played, a group can more fully understand the problem. Role-playing, for example, can be used to facilitate the case problem approach to discussion. In discussing case problem 2 on page 164, a group may decide that to solve the problem the superintendent should call the doctor and tell him to give Mary a tetanus shot. At this point, the instructor might step in and say, "All right, class, let's see how well that solution will work. Joan would you play the role of the doctor? And Fred, how about you being the superintendent who is going to make the call?"

Selecting a Role-Playing Problem
The problems below have been prepared with today's college student in mind. Additional problems may be developed by members of a group in a discussion situation, or by individual students as part of a class assignment.

One final note: After engaging in role-playing these problems, allow time for those in the audience to give their views and reactions to the drama.

1. A student who is of legal age is asked by his friends to buy the liquor for a weekend beach party. He knows he can get charged with contributing to the delinquency of minors if he is caught. He also wants to keep the status he has among his friends. What should the student do?

2. A new employee in a plant has a mother who must have open-heart surgery. She lives in another state, and the employee would like to take a four-day leave of absence to be with her. The plant is behind in filling orders and everyone is working a seven-day week. How should the employee handle the situation?

3. The students in an English class feel that the instructor assigns an excessive amount of homework each day. The instructor is teaching the course for the first time. How should the students handle the situation?

4. A student who will graduate in three weeks is offered a job that will start on the morning of his last exam. His instructor has indicated that he will give no early or makeup exams. What should the student do?

5. A secretary has recently begun a new job for an insurance company. The fringe benefits are excellent, the pay is good, but she runs into a problem. Her immediate supervisor is constantly making advances toward her that she resents. How should she handle the situation?

6. A first-year bank employee has been late for work an average of two or three times a week for the last month. His wife, who is in the hospital, will remain there for at least another week. The reason he has been late is that he has to feed, dress, and drive his three school-age children to school each day. His supervisor has called him in to talk about his tardiness. How should the bank employee handle the situation?

Additional Suggestions for Role-Playing
1. You have just graduated and are being interviewed for your first job.
2. A persistent salesman refuses to leave when you tell him to.
3. A policeman is about to ticket your car as you arrive on the scene.
4. A clerk who waited on you fifteen minutes ago now refuses to accept a return because you misplaced the receipt.
5. A teacher wrongfully accuses you of cheating.
6. A friend denies that he owes you $20.

Participating in Discussion

To a great extent, successful discussion depends on the participants. Sometimes discussions fail because the participants have little knowledge of the subject and, consequently, little to offer in solving the problem. At other times a discussion ends in aimless argument because of the inflexibility or refusal to compromise. Breakdowns in communication, an unfriendly atmosphere, and a tendency to stray from the subject also contribute to the failure of discussion. Effective participation in discussion requires both ability and understanding. Following are the duties of a participant in a discussion:

Listen Carefully

Critical listening is essential to effective discussion. It is an active process requiring both attention and concentration. All too often discussants respond to what they "thought" someone meant. If you are unclear as to the meaning of something that was said during a discussion, say so before the discussion continues.

Be Prepared

Every member of a discussion has a responsibility to be well informed on the topic being discussed. This means that if you have little knowledge of the subject, you spend time and effort researching it. If you are delivering a lecture or are a member of a symposium panel, prepare and practice your speech carefully so that you can deliver it extemporaneously with good eye contact.

Be Spontaneous

Participate whenever you have something relevant to say. Although you must not interrupt another speaker, if you have something important to say, interject it when there is a pause in the conversation. A relevant comment in the right place can often save the group time.

Share the Spotlight

Although you should participate when you have a worthwhile contribution, don't monopolize the discussion. Group thinking can be thought of as thinking out loud. Unless all members contribute, the full value of their knowledge and experience will not be brought to bear on the problem.

Be Friendly

The old saying "You catch more flies with honey than with vinegar" is especially appropriate to the group discussion situation. Group discussion requires flexibility and compromise. It is unlikely that either will occur in a hostile atmosphere.

Be Cooperative

Participants in group discussion must put the best interests of the group above their own personal interests. The goal of discussion is to arrive at a solution acceptable to all members of the group. This means that group members must be willing to work cooperatively to avoid conflict.

Be Objective

In order for a discussion to be successful each member must approach the question in an unbiased, objective way. If for some reason you have a strongly held attitude that would prevent you from discussing a topic objectively, excuse yourself from the discussion group.

Stick to the Point

Few things are more frustrating to a group than when a member introduces material that is completely off the subject. It is every member's responsibility to keep the discussion on track. Always be aware of where the discussion is heading and contribute only when your remarks are pertinent.

Use Time Wisely

A discussion participant should avoid belaboring a point. Once agreement is reached in regard to some aspect of the problem, move on. To explain to the group why you made the same decision as another member is counter-productive.

Speak Clearly

Unless the listener understands the message, communication does not take place. If you want to be understood, articulate your words carefully and pronounce them correctly. Speak with adequate volume and emphasize important points so that the other members of the group know exactly where you stand.

Be Natural

No matter which form of discussion you are involved in, be yourself. Speak in a conversational manner with which you feel comfortable. If you try to change your way of speaking, you are liable to sound stilted and unnatural.

Moderating the Discussion

Most discussion forms require a moderator. Seven specific duties of a moderator are listed here:

1. Start the discussion by introducing the topic and the lecturer or discussion participants to the audience.
2. Direct the discussion by seeing to it that the subject is adequately discussed and that the group moves steadily toward a solution or conclusion.
3. Encourage participation. Members who do not take part in the discussion contribute little or nothing to the outcome.
4. Resolve conflicts by using tact and diplomacy to minimize tension.

5. Control the time to make sure all aspects of the problem are discussed.
6. Provide transitions and summaries to help participants see what has been accomplished and what remains to be done.
7. Take charge of the forum period. Field all questions, rephrasing when necessary.

A Pattern for Problem Solving

Identifying the Problem

The first step in problem-solving discussion is to have the members pinpoint the problem. Many discussions fail because the problem is not clearly understood by all. Next, the problem must be carefully worded. When wording the problem for discussion, the group should adhere to the following guidelines:

1. The problem should be worded in the form of a question. A properly worded question holds up a problem in such a way as to motivate discussants to seek solutions to it.
2. It should be phrased to avoid a yes or no answer. Participants who answer yes or no to a question often feel committed to defend that answer. The result is that what started out as objective discussion turns into subjective debate.
3. It should be stated in an impartial way. A discussion question should never indicate bias. The question, When will we stop the stupid sale of handguns? is prejudiced. It would be far better to ask, How can the sale of handguns be effectively regulated?
4. It should be worded specifically. The question, What should the government do to prevent terrorism? is far too vague. Which government are we talking about? Where will the terrorism take place? A better question would be, What steps should the federal government take to prevent terrorists from illegally entering the United States?
5. It should be sufficiently restricted. The question, What should be done to stop world hunger? is so broad that it could not be adequately covered in a set period of time. A better question would be, What should be done to stop hunger in Detroit?

Analyzing the Problem

After identifying and wording the problem, the nature and causes of the problem should be explored. The group should consider such questions as these: What is the history of the problem? How serious is it? Who is affected by it? What are the causes?

The process of analysis usually requires research. Participants should research the discussion problem just as they would research the topic for a speech. A thorough investigation of the problem will give discussants a clear understanding of what conditions need correcting.

The final step in analysis is to decide on guidelines to evaluate proposed solutions. These guidelines should be agreed upon before possible solutions are proposed. A typical list of guidelines might include: it must be safe; it must be affordable; it must be obtainable; and it must not create new problems.

Finding the Best Solution

At this point members of the group should suggest possible solutions. It is a good idea to identify as many solutions as possible before evaluating any of them. An effective way to compile an adequate list of solutions is by using a technique called brainstorming.

In a discussion the brainstorming technique can be handled in two ways. The first is to have members of the group write down whatever solutions come to mind as quickly as they can. They should jot them down in phrases or sentences without evaluating them. After five minutes the exercise stops, and each list of solutions is read aloud. The second technique has one member of the group proposing a solution, another posing a different one, and so on. The brainstorming continues for a set period of time or until the group has no more solutions to offer. One member should be assigned to write down all the ideas.

Once a list of solutions has been established, the group can quickly eliminate any that are illogical or repetitive. The remaining solutions can then be evaluated according to the guidelines established earlier. It is wise for the group to evaluate each solution on the list before making their choice.

Finally, the group should make every effort to reach agreement as to the best solution or solutions. If they cannot reach a consensus, a majority vote should be taken.

Actuating the Solution

Once the group has agreed on a solution, it is necessary to take action. This might mean drafting a letter and sending it to the appropriate representatives in Washington, framing a petition and collecting signatures, or planning and staffing a fund-raising event. Perhaps the proposed solution will take the form of an oral report to the mayor and city council or to your instructor and the rest of the class. Sometimes a solution will require a written report. Whatever action is taken, the last job the group has is to implement the solution it chooses.

Evaluating Discussions

The discussion rating forms shown in Figures 12-1 and 12-2 are designed for both student and instructor evaluation. They list the characteristics to be considered when evaluating a discussion.

Using Case Problems

The best way to develop ability in group discussion is through guided practice. The use of case problems as discussion questions is an effective way of

DISCUSSION RATING FORM (GROUP)	Names	(John M.)	(Mary S.)	(Robert R.)	(George S.)
Scale: 1 superior / 2 above avg. / 3 average / 4 poor					
Participation–Listened carefully; was prepared; was spontaneous; used pertinent information; tested the thinking of others.					
Attitude–Was friendly, tactful, cooperative, flexible, objective.					
Thought Progression–Spoke to the point; stayed on the subject; used time wisely.					
Communicative Skills–Used adequate volume; was clear; was conversational; observed the rules of grammar.					

Overall Rating for Group_____

Comments:

FIGURE 12-1   Discussion Rating Form: Group

Discussion Rating Form (Individual)

Presentation by _____ Date _____

Grade _____

1. Participation

    A. Listened carefully

    B. Was prepared

    C. Was spontaneous

    D. Used pertinent information

    E. Tested thinking of others

2. Attitude

    A. Friendly

    B. Tactful

    C. Cooperative

    D. Flexible

    E. Objective

3. Thought Progression

    A. To the point

    B. Stayed on the subject

    C. Used time wisely

4. Communicative Skills

    A. Adequate volume

    B. Was clear

    C. Conversational

    D. Observed rules of grammar

Comments

FIGURE 12-2   Discussion Rating Form: Individual

stimulating this practice. These problems are typical of those that occur in everyday life and are the kinds of situations you are likely to encounter at school, at work, or at home.

There are no "right" or "wrong" solutions to these problems. However, each problem is constructed in such a way that choosing a solution poses a dilemma. For each problem there are two alternative solutions, both of which are undesirable. The job of the group is to choose the solution they see as being the least undesirable.

Remember, the group should make an effort to reach agreement on a solution for each problem. If they cannot reach a consensus, the solution should be chosen by majority opinion.

Case Problems*

1. You are a production foreman in an automotive parts fabricating plant. Company policy regarding credit given for employees' suggestions is to reward the first person who turns in a useful suggestion in written form. John has developed an idea concerning a manufacturing problem. He is ready to write it and turn it in, but George, a second employee, learns of the idea and turns in the written suggestion before John. As the foreman, these facts are known to you. Because the idea is a very useful one, you should reward one of the employees.

What should you do?

2. Mary F., who works in a sewing factory, ran a sewing machine needle through her finger. As superintendent of the factory, you sent her to the company doctor. He declared it was a clean wound and sent her back to work without giving her a tetanus shot as a precaution against lockjaw. The company is responsible for all expenses incurred by a worker in connection with a job-connected injury.

What should you do?

3. A few days before the final examination you learn by chance that another student in one of your courses has a copy of the questions to be used on the test and that he is passing it among his friends in the course. You know that several students in the course have already seen it and you suspect that nearly a third of those in the course have seen it.

What should you do?

4. John, a white student at a small out-of-state technical college, has fallen in love with Cindy, an African American student at the same school. He plans to invite her home for Christmas, but he does not plan to tell his parents

*Problems 1–3 are used with permission of the author from William E. Utterback, *Group Thinking and Conference Leadership*, rev. ed. (New York: Holt, Rinehart & Winston, Inc., 1964). Problems 4–19 have been taken with permission from Arthur Koch and Stanley B. Felber, *What Did You Say?* 3rd ed. (Englewood Cliffs, NJ: Prentice-Hall, 1985).

beforehand that she is African American. He argues that his parents have always insisted that they were unprejudiced, and now he will be able to see by their reaction if they are honest. Cindy does not agree.

What should John do?

5. Joan and Donna have been friends since childhood. Lately, Donna has been seeing a lot of an older, married man. Joan advises Donna to break this off, but Donna is convinced that the man plans to get a divorce and marry her. Donna has told her parents that she will be visiting Joan for the weekend so that she and the man can go off together.

What should Joan do?

6. When your college roommate returns from summer vacation he tells you he is engaged. When he shows you his fiancée's picture, you recognize her as a former classmate who has a reputation for being promiscuous. You like your roommate very much.

What should you do?

7. Julia is engaged to be married to Fred. The wedding is less than two months away, and Fred suggests that they begin their sexual relationship so that they can be sure that there are no physical or psychological barriers to a happy marriage. Julia believes very strongly that she should remain chaste before the wedding. Fred insists.

What should Julia do?

8. Ann has just found out from her family doctor that she has a venereal disease. The doctor asks her to reveal the name of the man involved so that he can be treated. Ann has had intercourse with two men, one of whom she plans to marry. She has no idea who gave her the disease.

What should she do?

9. While you are riding home with Ed, a good friend, he backs into a parked car, causing considerable damage. Although he has liability insurance, he declines to leave his name, explaining that he has already had two accidents this year, and that another will result in his insurance policy's cancellation. Ed drives you to and from work every day.

What should you do?

10. Harry and Tom are hometown neighbors and dormitory roommates in college. Tom is concerned because Harry has been experimenting with hard drugs which have seriously affected his schoolwork and his personality. Tom feels that something must be done before Harry becomes hopelessly addicted.

What should Tom do?

11. In 1966 John Graff was sentenced to life imprisonment for the murder of his business partner, Harry Fosdick. During his trial and imprisonment Graff had protested his innocence. He was released in April 1986 after serving the full twenty years at Joliet prison in Illinois and returned to Chicago, his hometown. Two days later he ran into Fosdick, the man he had been convicted of murdering. At this meeting, in the presence of witnesses, Fosdick admitted that he had intentionally framed Graff. The following day Fosdick was found murdered. When arrested for the crime, Graff admitted his guilt but claimed he was temporarily insane at the time.

What punishment, if any, should Graff get?

12. Henry, a rookie police officer, has been assigned to the vice squad temporarily to do undercover work. His job, for which he has grown a full beard, is to uncover prostitution. During his first night on the job he is propositioned by a woman he recognizes as the wife of a fellow police officer. Because of the beard she does not recognize him.

What should he do?

13. Penny Smith, a white coed, worked as a volunteer staff person for the political campaign of Wanda Jones, a young, idealistic African American woman. Wanda ran against George Alport, a member of the American Nazi party. Wanda won a narrow victory, which Penny, through involvement in the campaign, can prove was the result of voter fraud.

What should Penny do?

14. Sally and Bess have been best friends since childhood. Recently Bess has started a new job working in an office with Sally's husband Sam. She soon learns that Sam is having an affair with one of the secretaries. Bess believes that if Sally finds out it will destroy her marriage.

What should Bess do?

15. Fred's fifteen-year-old daughter, Ann, has recently begun a part-time job baby-sitting with his employer's young children. After her second night on the job she confides to Fred that the children have told her they are often beaten by their father. She says she has seen the marks of this abuse. She feels that the authorities should be notified. Fred is concerned about losing his job.

What should Fred do?

16. Paul writes very poorly in class. His essays indicate a lack of understanding of the simplest rules of grammar. The term paper that he hands in at the end of the semester is very well written and without error. The instructor suspects outside help but cannot prove it.

What should the instructor do?

17. Paul found what he believed were LSD tablets in his sister's room. When he questioned her about it, she insisted they were antibiotics for a cold. He has noticed that she has seemed unusually withdrawn lately. He has revealed all this to his parents who have told him not to let his imagination run away with him.

What should he do?

18. Don and Alice are required by law to take a blood test before marriage. During the examination it is discovered that Don has had a venereal disease. When Alice questions him about it, he refuses to answer her.

What should Alice do?

19. When visiting his friend Ralph for the weekend, Carl sees him take $10 from his mother's purse. On the following day Carl is present as the mother accuses Ralph's brother Tim of stealing the money. She punishes Tim by taking away his use of the car for one month.

What should Carl do?

20. Judy, a single parent, has recently moved to a small town to care for her widowed mother. Tim, her eight-year-old son, tells her that Scotty, his new friend, has contracted AIDS from a blood transfusion. There is only one grade school in town and school officials have made the decision to let Scotty stay in his and Tim's third-grade class. Judy is concerned because the two boys are inseparable companions and sometimes play together roughly.

What should she do?

21. Sara is engaged to Tom. The wedding is less than two months away when Sara finds out that Tom has spent three years in a federal prison. When she questions him about it he tells her that he doesn't want to talk about it because he was a victim of mistaken identity. Sara is concerned because he had not revealed this to her.

What should she do?

22. Ann and Randy are living together and plan to be married. One day, Ann's brother Keith walks into a gay bar to use the telephone. As he leaves, he notices Randy sitting in a corner booth holding hands with another male patron. He realizes that if he tells Ann she will be devastated. However, he is deeply aware of the high incidence of AIDS among bisexuals.

What should Keith do?

23. Joy and Natalie have been friends since childhood. On the following Saturday, Natalie will be the maid of honor at Joy's wedding. After the rehearsal dinner Joy's husband-to-be drives Natalie home because her car won't start. When he parks in front of her apartment, he touches her indecently. When she resists his advances, he begs her not to tell Joy.

What should Natalie do?

24. Mary and Beth shared an apartment for two years. During that time Beth confided to Mary that she had contracted herpes. Now Mary is carpooling with a fellow worker who has become romantically involved with Beth. He tells Mary that he is seriously considering moving in with Beth. Mary is concerned that Duane is unaware of Beth's disease.

What should she do?

25. Sandy and Kim have been best friends since childhood. A year ago Kim married and moved to another town. When Sandy visits her for two weeks during the summer, she discovers that Kim is being physically abused by her husband. One evening after Kim had been severely beaten, Sandy tells Kim that she is going to report her husband to the police. Kim begs her not to, claiming that he only hits her when he's been drinking. Sandy is afraid that if this continues Kim will be killed.

What should she do?

The Job Interview

After you graduate, probably the most crucial interview you will have is the job interview. This interview can provide the means for entering the job market, a way of gaining promotion, or a way of changing positions. Consequently, job interviewing skills can be important to you throughout your career.

Your goal in a job interview is to make a good impression, to present your qualifications to the interviewer in a clear, concise manner, and to convince him or her that you are the best applicant for the job. To do this effectively, you must prepare carefully. Following are step-by-step suggestions to plan for a successful interview:

Preparing to Be Interviewed

A successful interview can often have more to do with whether or not you are hired than your education, job qualifications, work experience, or recommendations. Therefore, it is in your best interests to plan for the interview carefully and thoroughly.

Self-Evaluation

It is very important for you to make a good first impression during your job interview, to have the interviewer see your best qualities. The question arises, "What is there about you that others will see as desirable?" Prior to the interview, it would be a good idea for you to evaluate yourself honestly and thoroughly. Most people have only a general picture of themselves. Few take the time for self-examination. Self-examination can give you a better picture of what and who you are and how others perceive you. Before the interview determine your strengths and weaknesses by asking yourself questions like these:

1. Am I satisfied with my physical appearance?
2. Do I get along with most people?

3. Am I intelligent?
4. Has my life been a good one?
5. Do the people who count listen to what I say?
6. Am I happy most of the time?
7. Do I make good decisions?
8. Am I changing positively?
9. Is my attitude positive?
10. Do I have a sense of humor?
11. Do I listen to others?
12. Is my health good?
13. Do I do things that count for something?
14. Can I make difficult decisions?
15. Do I let others know where I stand on an issue?
16. Am I organized?
17. Am I flexible?
18. Am I prejudiced?
19. Do I consider myself kind?
20. Do I like myself?

Written Materials

Almost as important as the interview itself are the written materials that accompany the interview. In order to set up the interview, you must send a letter of application for the job and a résumé to provide the recruiter with an indication of your interest in the job and some important background information about you before the interview takes place. The résumé and application letter should be tailored to the company and specific position for which you are applying. Immediately after the interview, you should send a letter of thanks to the interviewer for giving you the opportunity to interview for the job. When you hear from the company that you have been offered the job, you should respond with either a letter of acceptance or rejection. Sending these letters of thanks or acceptance/rejection have, for many, proven to be very effective. They underline your interest in the position and the company and are almost always filed under your name. Be aware that even if you aren't interested in a position with a certain company now, that might change in a few years.

Company Information

One of the first things to do when preparing for an interview is some background research on the company. This will provide you with information for answering questions during the interview and also give you insights for framing questions you might want to ask. Listed below are some suggestions for doing research on a prospective employer and the interviewer:

1. Determine salary range for this job or similar jobs.
2. Find out what the company manufactures or sells.
3. Check the business section of the local newspapers.
4. Ask the reference librarian for possible sources.
5. Call the public relations office of the company.
6. Check company catalogs and brochures.
7. Identify competitors.
8. Check company sales.
9. Ask someone in your school's placement office.
10. Check the company annual report.
11. Check with someone who works there.
12. Find the name and any information available about the interviewer.

Questions and Answers

The goal of the interviewer is to find out if you are the best applicant for the job opening. She will ask you a set of questions that will help her to arrive at that decision. If you can anticipate these questions and predetermine how you are going to answer them, chances are you will feel more at ease and do better in the interview. Below is a list of the most commonly asked questions at job interviews:

1. How did you learn about this job?
2. Why do you want to work for this company?
3. What qualifies you for this job?
4. What other jobs have you held?
5. What do you see yourself doing five years from now?
6. What do you see as your greatest strength?
7. What do you see as your greatest weakness?
8. What salary do you expect?
9. How do you spend your spare time?
10. In what school activities did you participate?
11. Are you willing to relocate to another city?
12. What hobbies or sports do you enjoy most?

Nonverbal Communication

Most experts in the communication field agree that up to 65 percent of the response you get from others is based on your nonverbal communication to them. Employers are interested in your appearance, your social skills, your ability to communicate, and your personality as well as your qualifications for the job. Small wonder since the number one reason for losing a job is the employee's inability to get along with others in the workplace. Because of this, the clothes you wear, your makeup and grooming, your mannerisms, and your personality all play a role in regard to the success of your interview. Below are some suggestions to follow when interviewing.

1. *Dress appropriately.* For some jobs casual wear might be appropriate—a dress shirt, slacks, and tie for men, and a skirt and blouse for women. However, for more prestigious positions, both men and women should dress conservatively. Men should wear suits and women skirted suits. Black, medium gray, or blue are good colors for the fall and winter months and brown or tan go well in spring and summer. Since getting a good job is important to you, you should invest in yourself. Buy clothes for the interview that are appropriate and have a look of quality. Avoid overusing makeup, cologne, or perfume.

2. *Create a good first image.* Arrive at the interview early. An early arrival will give the impression that you are eager to get the job. Be there at least fifteen minutes ahead of time. If you have to wait in the outer office, remember that a receptionist can often influence a decision of the interviewer. Be polite and friendly to both the receptionist and interviewer. Keep in mind that a smile, a friendly greeting, and an upbeat attitude can often be the difference between getting a job or not getting one.

When you walk into the interviewer's office do so briskly with a friendly expression on your face. Shake hands with the interviewer and when asked to be seated, lean forward in the seat to indicate both interest and attention. Answer all questions honestly and candidly. If you don't know the answer to a question, admit it rather than trying to fake it. The interviewer will appreciate your candor. When the interview is over, get up, walk over to the interviewer, shake hands again and thank him or her for the opportunity to interview. Leave the room as briskly and enthusiastically as when you entered.

Index